The 7
Most
Important
Questions
You'll Ever
Answer

Discovery House Publishers

Books, music, and videos that feed the soul with the Word of God

Box 3566 Grand Rapids, MI 49501

The 7
Most
Important
Questions
You'll Ever
Answer

Sparking Daily Renewal by
Defining the Issues That Really Matter

Daniel Henderson
with P. C. Roberts

Discovery House Publishers is affiliated with RBC
Ministries, Grand Rapids, Michigan 49512.

Discovery House books are distributed to the trade exclusively
by Barbour Publishing, Inc., Uhrichsville, OH 44683.

Unless indicated otherwise, Scripture is from the
New American Standard Bible. © 1960, 1962, 1968,
1971, 1972 Lockman Foundation. Used by permission.

Library of Congress Cataloging-in-Publication Data

Daniel Henderson with Patricia Roberts
   p. cm.
Includes bibliographical references.
ISBN 1-57293-034-9
1. Christian life. I. Roberts, Patricia (Patricia C.) II. Title.
BV4501.2.H3698   1998
248.4—dc21

                                   98-7249
                                   CIP

Printed in the United States of America

00 02 01 99
CHG
3 5 7 9 10 8 6 4 2

Contents

Dedication

To my parents: **James and Helen Henderson**

Dad, you are the most faithful, enduring, patient and caring man I know. Thank you for supporting me with such joy and loyalty. I had hoped Mom would have lived to read this book. But now in heaven, she doesn't need to. May these pages fill your heart with joy in your sadness, encouragement in your loneliness, and fulfillment in knowing that Mom and you gave me life—and taught me how to live.

To my "parents-in-love": **Fred and Vivian Brewer**

Thank you for your faithful example of 55 years of full-time ministry, for the gift of my wife, and for loving me with devotion beyond my wildest dreams.

Acknowledgments

I suppose many people dream of being an author. Over the years it has crossed my mind several times. Yet, the busy demands of raising a young family and the challenges of pastoral ministry never seemed compatible with spending a lot of time writing books.

I remember hearing a quote by Ray Stedman, who said that a person should not write a book until he is at least forty years old. Sensing the wisdom in his words, I have not aggressively pursued a writing ministry. Were it not for a team of people who had vision and a willing heart, this project would not have become a reality. As the Lord would have it, I turned forty just weeks before the publication of this book. God sure is faithful and timely!

His faithfulness and goodness has been seen in the following lives:

Pat Roberts—Whose interest, persistence, and expertise transformed my teaching series into a proposal and, eventually, a manuscript. Thank you Pat for your partnership in this ministry.

Barbara McGee and Gina McIntosh—My capable and conscientious office assistants who kept my life and the details of this project in order during some very busy days. Thanks for your hard work and endurance.

Cindy Woods and Cindy Turpin—Two wonderful and willing volunteers who transcribed this material from the original sermons. Your quiet efforts have blossomed into fruitful ministry.

The staff, elders, and congregation of Arcade Baptist Church— Your friendship, support, and responsiveness have provided the impetus and environment to take this challenge seriously.

Bob DeVries, Tim Beals, Jackie Phillips, and the team at Discovery House—Your willingness to include me in your fine family of authors is one of the greatest honors of my life.

Most of all . . .

Rosemary—my devoted and loyal wife. Thank you for your patience and for all of your encouragement to see this project through to completion.

Justin, Jordan, and Heather—my fantastic children. Thanks for letting dad hang out in his "prayer shed" with his computer for those many long hours. Even when I was working early and late on this book, I was thinking of you—with deep love and gratitude.

My Lord and Savior, Jesus Christ—Thank you, Lord, for being so willing to teach me Your truth and to form in me a life's-message that might touch the lives of others.

Daniel Henderson

Foreword

For most of us, life is lived in a whirlwind of activities. We go from event to event, day after day without much thought to the things that really matter. Daniel Henderson forces us to take a time-out and face the ultimate issues of life, death, and eternity. He confronts us with the questions that really matter.

Ministry is increasingly complex in a culture that is falling apart. Broken promises. Broken relationships. Broken families. Broken people. But the issues remain the same. These are the questions Daniel deals with in his book. They transcend circumstances and people. They are universal. They get to the heart of the matter.

Most of us are familiar with these questions, but we seldom take the time to ponder them in a deep way. Daniel helps us to do that. This book will trouble you. It will convict you, and, if you heed its advice, it will change you. Everybody, believer or not, ought to read and heed this book. It is a fresh approach to the age-old issues of human existence.

I have known Daniel for many years. We shared ministry together in the past. He has a passion for helping people and a passion for the Word of God. This book merges both of these passions. Thank you for writing this book!

Dr. Edward G. Dobson
Senior Pastor
Calvary Church
Grand Rapids, Michigan

Introduction

Choosing the Right Approach

A man said to the universe: "Sir, I exist!"
"However," replied the universe,
"The fact has not created in me
A sense of obligation."
Stephen Crane[1]

"The greatest battles of life are fought out daily
in the silent chambers of the soul."
David O. McKay[2]

He was the classic first-century example of a man who was climbing the ladder of success, only to find that it was leaning against the wrong wall. Everyone in his day knew him as Saul. Today, we remember him as Paul. His name change reflected a true transformation of identity. But that was only part of the story. What follows in these pages is a sort of explanation of the rest of his story. And mine. And, I trust, yours as well.

Saul was a driven man; passionate to get to the top. He was determined to succeed in his good cause; out to make a name for himself. One day this Jewish zealot was on the road again. This time, he was headed north to the city of Damascus. He was hot on the trail of some more of those "Christians" who had fled Jerusalem to escape his persecuting passion. Saul could not stand these people of "the way" who were posing a threat to his tightly organized world.

But it all changed in a flash—literally. An inexplicable bright light at mid-day left him on his face, blind and baffled. In that hour of crisis, he was confronted with the truth about what was wrong with his life and how he needed to change his ways. In the days that followed, he would contemplate answers to the most important questions he had ever asked.

In that defining moment of his life he asked, "Who are you, Lord?" (Acts 9:5 NKJV). And as naturally as "A" follows "B," he also inquired, "What do you want me to do?" (Acts 9:6 NKJV). The answers he discovered made all the difference in the world—his world and ours.

Today, the reality of Saul's quest is very much like ours. His ladder was the Jewish religion. Ours might be another religion—or the absence of one. His wall was self-righteous achievement. Ours might be anything from self-centeredness to self-actualization. While the names and cultures have changed, human hearts are still the same. Today, our roads aren't dusty. Instead, they are paved and jammed full of high-speed automobiles equipped with cellular phones. Under Paul's arm you might have found a tattered edition of the Hebrew scriptures. We usually carry a well-worn time-management binder. Still, we are moving fast down the same road of life—in desperate need of a defining moment to bring sense to our non-sense and meaning to our madness.

We all need a transformation like Paul's. With it will come a meaningful reason for living and clear direction for life. But it all begins, as it did with him, by asking the right questions and getting answers from the right source. Then we can set up a new ladder against the right wall, on a foundation of lasting truth. That's why this book was written.

Asking the right questions to find the right answers

Our quest for meaning drives us to ask many questions and propose many answers, but we end up with few sound conclusions. Some tell us that management of our time, money, and relationships is the answer to "getting it all together." We buy sophisticated leather-bound time-organizers, with the intention of inserting neatly lined weekly, daily, and hourly pages. In an attempt to systematically track the way we spend our limited resources, we obediently fill in little squares. Still, for lack of a firm foundation, the bottom keeps dropping out of our lives.

This quest for significance fuels the market for the various efficiency and personal fulfillment formulas that continually appear on bestseller book lists. We faithfully attend seminars, study the latest organizational techniques, and carve out precious time to sit at the feet of any person willing to share a successful "how-to". Yet, at the end of the year, month, week, or day, we still have the feeling that something is missing. And it is.

So many of the self-improvement and goal-setting books lack meaningful integration for a life journey with purpose. They may enable us to look impressive on the outside, but things eventually decline into disarray and despondency on the inside.

Sometimes we are like Joe, a character out of a *Reader's Digest* story, who had ordered an expensive suit for a banquet. As Joe left the tailor's shop, a sudden rainstorm doused the jacket and shrank one of the sleeves.

"We can't do anything about it today," the tailor told Joe when he returned to the shop. "Just stretch the sleeve over your hand, and no one will notice."

With his arm contorted, Joe left the shop, and again was doused by rain. This time, a pant leg shrank.

"I can't take care of that now!" exclaimed the tailor. "Pull the bottom of the pants over your heel, and nobody will notice."

His body twisted, Joe again left the shop. Two women were passing by.

"That poor man!" said one. "I wonder what's wrong with him?"

"I don't know," said the other. "But he sure is wearing a nice suit!"[3]

In the busyness of adapting and contorting to daily demands and popular theories, we've forgotten to consider that God has a plan for us. It's an itinerary with a perfectly tailored purpose that includes hope and a future. Not found in our leather-bound, form-filled organizer or in any other time-management technique is the "why" and "where" of what God says about Himself and His plans for us.

God's better idea for you

God has always had a better idea. Jeremiah 29:11 says: " 'I know the plans that I have for you,' declares the LORD, 'plans for welfare and not for calamity, to give you a future and a hope.' " He wants us to sink roots deep into the soil of His promises as we allow His truth to penetrate deeply into the core of our souls. Then we can trade in the frustration of our best efforts for the fulfillment of His efforts in and through us. Only then do the pieces begin to fit together.

Perhaps you've been feeling like Alice in Wonderland when she said, "If you don't know where you're going, any road will get you there." When we forget God's plan, our well-executed, organized road often leads us back to the same old spot where we are empty and ineffective. Most people—even those who claim to be Christians—have no idea of the why or where they are going once they accomplish their objectives. Yet, we keep going through the motions because it seems to be the thing to do.

You only go around once in life— grab all of the reality you can

While in college, four fellow students and I made a summer ministry trek across the country. One evening, while ministering at a church in a Seattle suburb, our team was invited to visit a Boeing facility. Our host was a graveyard shift supervisor who offered to let us operate a 747 cockpit simulator.

What an experience! The controls were complicated and the techniques required for piloting this mammoth plane were far beyond our abilities.

In a simulated cruise over Seattle, I flew right through a high-rise bank building, then proceeded to crash into Mount Rainier. While landing, I effectively demolished one of the large runway hangars. Fortunately, it was all pretend. Otherwise, none of us would have survived the tumultuous mishaps brought on by my reckless maneuvers and amateur explorations.

Many people live life as if flying a simulator. They create their own imaginary worlds, hoping to avoid the real consequences of ignorant and purposeless action. If the journey can be punctuated with just enough thrills, all will turn out well. If the visual screen can be kept active and the volume loud enough, the real world of empty existence may never materialize. Successfully minimize pain and eventually our planes may land on the happy fields of retirement.

But life is not a simulator. Uninformed choices bring fatal spiritual and emotional consequences. Without the right approach, we crash and burn.

It's time to take modern life-management blueprints back to the drawing board. We need a firm foundation that has roots deep in the soil of time and history. Gimmicks, fads, and techniques that lack biblical wisdom have to be replaced with a firm footing on a rock-solid base. Our lives need to be transformed—a change powerful enough to alter our lives and renew our minds based on God's enduring truth.

Strategic daily renewal

The hardest thing about the Christian life is that it is so *daily*. David O. McKay reiterates this idea when he says, "The greatest battles of life are fought out daily in the silent chambers of the soul."[4]

Life is daily, and because it is, we must make the most of the time God gives us. Dr. Tom Morris, in his book *True Success*, says, "Too many people seem to wander through life like sleepwalkers, meandering from day to day, week to week, year to year. Each day they get up, they get dressed, they eat, they fall into some familiar routines, engaging in various forms of activity or inactivity. They eat again, and then again, filling time in between, undress, go back to bed, and then hours later begin the whole cycle once more over and over and over and over . . . ."[5]

We have to break the cycle of misspent and misguided daily living. Every day is significant in the battle of life, and each one must be seized with a renewal that puts us on the winning side.

Our physical bodies can soon become ill without proper care and nutrition. A tidy house can become a pigpen with just a few days of neglect. A marriage can become troubled after just a few episodes of anger and misunderstanding. An automobile not properly maintained can break down right in front of the gas station or service center. In the same way, our lives can break down without daily guidance and renewal in God's provision.

Efficiency is doing things right. Effectiveness is doing the right things.

In today's flooded market of personal time-management tools and self-help techniques, there's a big difference between being efficient and being effective. Efficiency is doing things right. It's accomplished by scheduled planning. Effectiveness is doing the right things. This requires wisdom and understanding—leading to a realization of the Jeremiah principle (29:11).

Life at the crossroads

If we forget to consider God's plans for us, it's just a matter of time before we find ourselves at those inevitable four crossroads: Directionless, Disjointed, Distracted, and Discouraged lives.

Directionless lives

For most Americans, life is experienced at high speed. The demands of going to work, caring for a family, volunteering in the community, serving at church, maintaining the car, repairing the house, paying the bills, answering the e-mail, and trying to find leisure, combine to push us beyond the speed limit. We go to bed with our "to do" lists full of undone tasks. As we doze off to sleep, we feel this haunting sense that we will never get on top of things. The alarm goes off the next morning. We quickly shower, eat, and rush off to the races saying to ourselves, "I've got to get going." Perhaps we would do well to ask, "Where am I going?" and "Why am I in such a hurry to get there?" Without a solid foundation of truth, an integration of the vital issues of life, and a consistent renewal of our minds in these realities, we will tend to be like the cowboy riding off into the sunset—going nowhere in particular.

Disjointed lives

Life can soon begin to feel like a jigsaw puzzle that's missing some pieces. We have our daily or hourly time-management binder over here, our Bible in the corner, inspirational books over there, and lists of goals, priorities, and values scattered here and there (given that we have written some of them down).

In the midst of this, we attempt to formulate a mission statement for life. Feeling insecure, we sense that the puzzle pieces never really fit together with the reality of how we live. That's disturbing and distracting.

Distracted lives

Margaret Fuller once said, "Men, for the sake of getting a living, forget to live."[6] Today, for both men and women, securing a living is much more complex than it used to be. There are so many distractions pulling at us—so many options and choices.

In America, where two hundred new products are introduced each week, even going to the grocery store results in frustration. It used to be simple to purchase a box of cereal. Now we choose according to color, promotional offer, size, nutritional value, price. So many choices.

Every year, over two hundred new magazines are introduced. At restaurants, menus change as the list of food and drink options continues to grow.

I remember hearing a story about the plight of a foreign exchange student who had recently come to America. He went to his professor for advice on how to order food in restaurants. Since he didn't speak English fluently, and was still learning about our culture, the professor suggested that he just go in, sit down, and say, "Hamburger, Coke, fries."

"Men, for the sake of getting a living, forget to live."

Every time he went to a restaurant, he said, "Hamburger, Coke, fries." After two months, he was sick of having a hamburger, Coke, and fries. Returning to the professor, he shared his problem.

The professor said, "Do you like breakfast?" When the student said "yes," he was told to try ordering eggs, toast, and juice.

The next morning, sitting in the restaurant, he ordered "Eggs, toast, and juice."

"Great," replied the waitress. She wrote it down and then asked, "Now, how would you like your eggs? Fried, poached, over easy, firm, scrambled, sunny-side up? And what about your toast? Wheat, white, rye; or would you like a muffin, bagel, or breakfast roll? And juice. You have a choice of orange, apple, grapefruit, pomegranate."

The student looked at her and said, "Hamburger, Coke, fries."

Don't you sometimes wish that life could be reduced to hamburger, Coke, and fries?

Discouraged lives

When we lack direction, are bombarded by distractions, and feel disjointed, we become discouraged. It's like comedian Lewis Grizzard said, "Life is like a dogsled team. If you ain't the lead dog, the scenery never changes."[7] Some of us feel like the second dog in a dogsled team, seeing the same old thing, and wondering, *What am I doing with my life?*

The circular pattern that sometimes characterizes our experience of life could well be summarized by the reflections of an immigrant sewer worker in the Chicago area when he said, "I digge de ditch to gette de money to buye de food to gette de strength to digge de ditch."[8]

Thinking deeply about the things that drive us

Reflecting on life reminds me of Rodin's famous sculpture, *The Thinker.* I remember seeing the old black-and-white clips of this statue in the opening footage of the Dobie Gillis show. Perhaps you've seen small-scale reproductions of the nude male statue, sitting on a rock with his chin on his fist, deep in thought. And the obvious question is, *What is he thinking about?* One of the common guesses is, *I wonder where I left my clothes?*

For some of us, that's about as deep as we get. Our most pressing questions for the day are: Where did I leave those car keys? What will we have for dinner tonight? Is it payday yet? Even for people who are familiar with biblical wisdom, we get so busy with all of life's trivial things that we forget to ask and answer the important questions that could lead to significant changes in the way we live.

The people who have made the greatest difference in the world have not necessarily been the smartest, best-looking, most talented, or wealthy. They are the people with deeply held beliefs, for better or worse. Anyone from Aristotle to Jefferson, from Mao to Marx, from Joan of Arc to Gandhi to

. . . you name them. These people's lives were driven by their convictions.

From the flames that killed her, Joan of Arc's words still speak: "Every man gives his life for what he believes, and every woman gives her life for what she believes. Sometimes people believe in little or nothing, and yet they give their lives to that little or nothing. One life is all we have; we live it and it's gone. But . . . to live without belief is more terrible than dying, even more terrible than dying young."[9]

The pensive posture of *The Thinker* seems to illustrate what Joan of Arc said. The man that the statue represents apparently had convictions and beliefs worth thinking about. And that's where we start.

The integrity-driven life

We are all driven by something, it seems. For some it is greed. For others it may be fame, domination, or fear. Some tremendous writers have challenged us to think about what drives us. In some cases we are urged to a life driven by clear values. Others offer the importance of a defined purpose to motivate and guide our lives. The "management-by-objectives" gurus focus us on the role of goals and planning.

Real integrity makes us whole people. It speaks of lives that are complete, where all the pieces fit together.

*

These all contribute to our thinking in valuable ways. However, I have always found a need to fit all of these vital pieces together in a clear, synthesized approach to daily life. What would happen if we could integrate the best that has been offered to us into a daily plan for enduring personal renewal? What if we based all of this on some very clear thinking about God? This would be an "integrated" life. Maybe we could call it an integrity-driven life.

The word *integrity*, from the Latin root, *integer*, signifies a whole number. Likewise, real integrity makes us whole people. It speaks of lives that are complete, where all the pieces fit together. Stephen Carter notes in his book, *Integrity*, that it is "not the frenzy of a fanatic who wants to remake all the world in a single mold but the serenity of a person who is confident in the knowledge that he or she is living rightly." [10]

Questions, answers, and the integrated life

We're going to think about the seven most important questions you will ever be asked. The first one will help you lay an unshakable foundation for your life's journey, while the other six will give you a map that bypasses the crossroads of a directionless and disheartened destination.

These questions have to do with life, a defined life. We're going to travel in the direction of a meaningful life—one of significance, a life where there is a vision of who we are to be. We're talking about a life of integrity.

Is that the kind of life you have? Does it all fit and work together? A favorable response can be found when you consider the seven most important questions you'll ever answer: Who is God? Who am I? Why am I here? What really matters? What shall I do? How shall I do it? When shall I do it?

These questions deal with issues of theology, identity, purpose, values, priorities, goals, and the use of time. We're going to start with theology, because everything begins with God, including time-management.

Building blocks for daily integration

It all begins with God

The aspiration to live a meaningful life begins with theology. Everyone has a theology, whether they call it that or not. And everyone ultimately lives according to their basic belief system. So the first question, "Who is God?" is crucial if one's foundation is going to withstand the earth-shaking changes that come in life.

Next up: identity

From this base, we explore answers to the question we sometimes ask while looking in the mirror: "Who am I?" As with our theology, we also ultimately live out our identity. For many, identity is shaped by inputs that are temporary. It is often based on how we can perform or what people say or think about us. Lily Tomlin said it this way: "I always wanted to be *somebody*. I should have been more specific."[11] At this very moment, we are all living out our identity, whether we've thought about it or not.

Living "on purpose"

Next, "Why am I here?" Some of us say, when the alarm goes off, "Good Lord, it's morning." Instead, we ought to get up, saying, "Good morning, Lord! I know why I'm here and what I'm all about." How does a person, facing the dawn of each new day, incorporate this perspective? Some find the answer to that question by realizing that their only true happiness comes when they are spending themselves on some truth-based, meaningful purpose.

The guiding principles

That brings us to the fourth question: "What really matters?" The answer to this question is determined by the values you choose, consciously or unconsciously, in your daily life.

How do you know what these core beliefs are? Try examining your daily choices. Your actions reveal your convictions.

Most of us are unaware of how frequently core precepts shape our daily decisions. What is even more disturbing, most people don't even know—or seem to care about—what their core beliefs are. It's disturbing because our philosophy of life eventually brings us face to face with our real priorities.

Two of my favorite philosophers, Lucy and Linus, were getting ready to pull a chicken wishbone apart, each one making a wish. With her usual take-charge attitude, Lucy explained that the one who ended up with the largest part of the wishbone would have a wish come true.

"Do I have to say the wish out loud? " asked Linus.

"Of course. If you don't say it out loud it won't come true," replied Lucy. So she went ahead and wished for a new bike, skates, four sweaters, a new dress, and one hundred dollars.

Linus said, "I wish for a long life for all of my friends, I wish for world peace, I wish for great advancements in medical research."

Lucy took the wishbone and threw it away. "Linus," she said, "that's the trouble with you. You're always spoiling everything."[12]

Our values are a system of principles, a set of integrated convictions. Until you know what really matters, it will be difficult to know what you should be doing. Not knowing "what" to do keeps you from knowing "how" to successfully do it.

The power of priorities

When you know what really matters, the next question is, "What should I do?" Peter Drucker, the well-known business consultant, says, "There are really only two questions to ask yourself; that is, what is my business, and number two, how's business?" Pretty simple? Many of us need to ask these questions instead: "What am I doing with my life, and how am I doing?" These two questions address the fundamental issue of priorities.

Do you see how the seven questions build upon one another? First, there is the foundational base of your own personal theology. Next, the understanding of who you are. These questions are seldom addressed in life-planning techniques, yet they form an indispensable basis for deciding how to manage your time.

From there we seek to discern your unique purpose and what really matters. Answers to these questions will guide you to use time wisely, according to your personal convictions and purpose.

When you aren't sure about what to do, much less how to do it, then it doesn't matter when you do it. How can you manage time, or anything else, when you don't know where you are going?

Going for good goals

After deciding what to do comes the question: "How should I do these things I value?" Here's where we deal with the issue of goals. Goals are specific, measurable plans for accomplishment—well-conceived specific plans for accomplishing our objectives.

These detailed plans are what most organizational books emphasize. They urge us to set a goal and go for it, to actualize ourselves and achieve our dreams. But based upon what? We need to know the "what" and "why" before we ever start down this path.

Living in time

The final question is, "When should I do it?" This time-management issue, placed well after a firm foundation is established, can be decided only after these other six important questions are asked and answered. However, it is neither the ultimate goal nor the final destination.

If we were to illustrate this question-and-answer process, it would look like this:

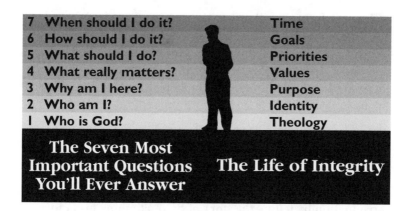

7	When should I do it?	Time
6	How should I do it?	Goals
5	What should I do?	Priorities
4	What really matters?	Values
3	Why am I here?	Purpose
2	Who am I?	Identity
1	Who is God?	Theology

The Seven Most Important Questions You'll Ever Answer **The Life of Integrity**

Beginning with the *ultimate* end in mind

In his best-selling book, *The Seven Habits of Highly Effective People*, Steven Covey advocates "beginning with the end in mind."[13] He urges us to rehearse our own funerals. What will our family, friends, and acquaintances say about us? What will we want noted in the eulogy? The answers to these questions provide the mark for which we aim, according to Covey.

But in reality, that imaginary vision of "the end" is short-sighted. The grave is not our final resting place. Death is like a doorway—for better or for worse, through it, we enter into eternity. According to the Scripture, entering into eternity will end our earthly journey, and we will find ourselves in either blissful fellowship with God or forever separated from His presence (1 Thessalonians 4:13–17; 2 Thessalonians 1:5–10).

Even in heaven, our earthly deeds will determine our rewards, or lack of them. Therefore, the comments that matter most are not the reflections of mourners at a funeral. What ultimately matters is the final evaluation of the God who created us and designed a plan for our lives.

To truly begin with the end in mind, we must realize that what we do with our earthly minutes and hours definitely influences how we will spend the rest of eternity. We seek to ask and answer these seven most important questions so that we will consider the impact of our existence "beyond the doorway." In doing this, we have the opportunity to live fully integrated with the future and the hope that God has planned for us.

Your ladder, your life, and your eternity

So, this journey is really about eternity and its connection with the here and now. You will remember that we began this introduction by telling the story of Saul, climbing his ladder of "success" based on a foundation of self. In his journey we see a mirror of our own temporal pursuits. In the ultimate analysis, this life-paradigm is faulty. The rungs of the ladder are attractive, but unreliable. The wall against which our ladder is leaning will ultimately crumble. Often, it looks like this:

Instead, we need a new ladder, a new foundation, and a new wall. For Saul, this great exchange occurred, by God's grace, as he came to terms with the deep questions of his soul. The challenge of this book is to trade in a ladder of success for a ladder of integrity, like the one shown here.

With God's enabling, you can base your life's pursuit on the firm bedrock of truth, and prop it against the wall of eternal significance. Let the ideas in this book assist you with your daily climb. The discoveries we make together will provide a foundation and focus for a life of true fulfillment.

Journeying together on the pathway of discovery

Having laid out the approach for this book in rapid-fire fashion, let me pull up a stool for a brief heart-to-heart chat before we begin this journey together. For me to say that I have mastered these questions would leave a false impression. It's been said that anyone who knows all the answers just isn't up-to-date on the questions. I certainly do not have all the answers. Yet, I am trying to stay up-to-date on these important questions of life. It is my hope and prayer that every day of my life this integrated approach marks the way I think and live.

Nearly every week someone tells me about the great impact these questions have made on his or her experience. And whenever I counsel church members seeking answers to stressful situations, I have found that these questions have helped bring clarity and direction. The approach has proven to be productive and beneficial. Thus, this book.

These questions, and the answers we discover together, will not solve every problem or make life a bastion of perfection. But they will determine a course, provide a framework, and point to the meaning God has assigned to every facet of life. When taken seriously, they will bring fundamental biblical truths into a process for living that will mark you, and prepare you for eternity.

My hope is that in the course of reading this book we will find ourselves on a "Damascus Road" of sorts, asking important questions, discovering powerful answers, and finding ourselves changed just like the apostle Paul did.

From irritation to illumination

In a recent leadership conference, Jim Collins, former Stanford professor and author of *Built To Last*, described his goal as a teacher. He said his job is to offer thought-provoking ideas and to leave people with "grains of sand in their minds." These ideas create such an irritation that over time, through great thought and contemplation, they become pearls of wisdom.

This book is designed to leave in your mind grains of truth that produce wisdom you will use every day. The questions are designed to be delightfully provocative. And while the answers aren't always easily achieved, they are clearly worth the energy. Serious consideration will invariably form pearls of discovery that will result in a more integrated life than ever before. The precious effort and valuable time invested will prove profitable—both for now and eternity.

Just as the apostle Paul found answers that changed his life and his world, may your answers lead you into a transformed life shaped by the truths of God's Word.

Question 1

"Who is God?"

*Wrong ideas about God are not only the fountain
from which the polluted waters of idolatry flow;
they are themselves idolatrous. The idolater simply imagines
things about God and acts as if they were true . . . .*
A.W. Tozer[1]

To believe in God is to "let God be God." This is the chief business of faith. As we believe, we are allowing God to be in our lives what He already is in Himself. In trusting God, we are living out our assumptions, putting into practice all that we say He is in theory so that who God is and what He has done can make the difference in every part of our lives.
Os Guinness[2]

It's been said that "there are no atheists in foxholes." I suppose this is true. As a baby-boomer who never enlisted in the military, I wouldn't know from personal experience. In fact, I've never really conversed with anyone who spent time in a foxhole. In my limited experience it is hard to imagine having your life on the line while shrapnel and grenades threaten your personal being. I suppose that the heat of the battle would be a hard time to deny the reality of eternity, and that a true and living God exists.

It is a sad thought, however. To think that someone could skip through life and not carefully consider one of life's most important questions until he or she was about to draw life's last breath seems a little crazy. Still, a lot of people do it.

This section is a call to dig down deep and visit your own personal philosophical foxhole of sorts. Why wait until time is running out on the countdown of your life to give careful thought to the reality of God? Why not begin a quest to settle this absolutely essential issue as soon as possible? The foxhole in which one finds himself while in the confusion and smoke of a raging battle is usually not the best place to exert deliberate, life-changing concentration.

Now I know that the tendency of human nature is to procrastinate on the big and sometimes uncomfortable issues that await us on the journey of life. How many times have you crammed all night long because the reality of a final exam would confront you the next morning? Many of us wait for the wake-up call of shortness of breath or excruciating pain before we go

31

to see a doctor. How many times have you delayed flossing your teeth until the hour before that dental appointment?

Sometimes it is that sense of significant accountability that gets us going. Other times it is the undeniable scare of personal pain that moves us to get the answers we need. The truly wise person asks the important questions when he has the time and focus to find the right answers. You've got every reason to begin *now* to answer the question, "Who is God?" Dig your own fox-hole—during peacetime—and let the urgency of this question fill your thoughts and challenge your will.

This section is designed to challenge you to take a few moments to answer the question. To use another word picture—you'll be challenged to stop and put the dipstick of ruthless honesty into the oil well of your heart. My guess is that you will find some pain and low-level confusion that's been gurgling in the depths of your being for awhile. Even though you've kept your foot heavy on the accelerator of your life in recent days, the time will come when "that pain" will catch up to you and the ride will end. Why not take time now to get an answer before it's too late? Let's visit the foxhole together. It's time to think about God. So, grab a shovel and let's dig in. It will be time well spent.

The foundation for an integrated life

Have you ever considered that your ultimate approach to life-management is really an issue of theology? After all, the book of Proverbs tells us repeatedly that, "the fear of the LORD is the beginning of wisdom." Applying truth to daily life begins with understanding God.

Let's go slow here, since theology is not always a topic discussed during an early breakfast or in a casual conversation. For our purposes, we'll define *theology* simply as, "your view of God." Your view of God exerts a great deal of influence on you because ultimately, everyone lives out his or her belief about the existence and character of God.

One thing needs to be clear: It's not the question of "Who is God?" that becomes your foundation for life's journey. It's the answer to this question that determines your daily perspective on life and influences your decisions. That's why the question needs to be asked and answered.

What you think about when the word "God" comes to mind is the most important thing about you.

A.W. Tozer observed that what you think about when the word *God* comes to mind is the most important thing about you. It determines how you live your life. In the Bible, the psalmist referred to people who bow before lifeless idols and said, "those who make them will become like them, yes, everyone who trusts in them" (Psalm 135:18).

The first home my wife and I purchased was in the Seattle area. It was a new house. We were the first buyers in the neighborhood so we selected our lot, floor plan, and preferences for the various amenities. Of course, you can imagine that once construction began we drove by our "home-to-be" virtually every day. It seemed like they took forever digging the trenches and pouring the concrete to construct a complete and solid foundation. Many weeks later, as we watched them put the walls up, put on the roof, and finish the exterior and interior, we understood why the foundation was so very essential. A carelessly constructed or incomplete foundation would undermine the stability of the entire house. All of the fine, colorful carpentry, new windows, and fresh paint ultimately would have been for no purpose if the house crumbled due to a lousy foundation.

The same is true with our lives. We are often in such a hurry to build a career, carve out a destiny, and establish a family that we inadvertently ignore the bedrock issue of building life on a firm foundation. Establishing this foundation is crucial before going any further in life. It also requires a daily commitment. All of us must recognize the necessity of having a solid ground of truth. If you want a life that lasts, you must build your house on the rock (see Matthew 7:24–27).

Because of its importance, we're going to explore six major concepts of *God*. We'll also examine the foundation each belief provides. One of these views may describe your view of God or of theology.

The god of the atheist

Wise King Solomon said, "The fool has said in his heart, 'There is no God' " (Psalm 14:1). Some commentators view the fool's assertion as the words of the atheist who says, "No, God!" The coin of atheism has two sides. On an intellectual level, atheists seek to remove God from their thinking. On a volitional level, their heart's antagonism toward God requires denying His existence, rather than dealing with Him.

In my experience, most atheists tend to deny God's existence because some experience in life affected their notion of God and lead to a disappointment. They deny Him, not because of an intellectual decision, but because of an emotional reaction. Considering the idea that God exists evokes responses ranging from incredulous to repugnant. Such responses may be due to a bitter experience as a child or as an adult, or may indicate that an individual has constructed some kind of intellectual box over the years.

Whatever the reason, the atheist holds to the position that God doesn't exist. Consequently, the foundation of life becomes one's self. However, having yourself as your foundation is not worth building on at all. God said through the prophet Jeremiah, "Cursed is the man who trusts in mankind and makes flesh his strength, and whose heart turns away from the LORD" (Jeremiah 17:5). Atheism itself is the epitome of self-trust.

People who embrace the beliefs of Atheism make a foolish wager on eternity. A Christian mathematician named Blaise Paschal said, "If you are right in your belief that there is no God, then I have really lost nothing by believing. But, if I am right in believing that the God of the Bible exists, then you, my friend, have lost it all."

The following headstone inscription seems to capture how an atheist might view his burial: "Here lies an atheist, all dressed up, no place to go."

The god of the agnostic

Agnostics have a belief system that upholds the concept of "no knowledge." Its adherents say that one can't really know if God exists. C. S. Lewis, well-known author, was once an agnostic. He didn't think a person could ever be sure who God is or if He exists. That is, until Lewis came to terms with Jesus Christ.

In Acts 17:16–34, the apostle Paul addressed two groups of philosophers. Although neither of them were agnostics, those that refused to believe Paul's message exhibited an attitude not unlike that of the agnostic—"Ever learning but never able to come to a knowledge of the truth" (2 Timothy 3:7; Acts 17:21). Paul said to them, "Men of Athens . . . you are very religious. . . . I . . . found an altar with this inscription, 'To An Unknown God'. " If an agnostic were to build an altar and etch an inscription on it, he would probably choose this same inscription. An agnostic never really knows if God is there or how to understand Him.

Recently, I stood in the area called Mars Hill where Paul likely made his keen observations about the culture of his day.

Visiting Greece reminded me that, on one hand, everything about that historic site has changed. On the other hand, nothing has changed. The majesty of the Acropolis and the beauty of the Parthenon have certainly lost their luster and influence since the day when Paul stood in their shadows, exchanging ideas with the philosophers of his day. Yet, the cultural landscape of irreligious modern-day Greece still speaks of mankind's reluctance to give much attention to the notion of there being one true God. In that regard, Greece is like much of the world. Millions are content with thinking *Maybe there is a God, and maybe there isn't, but who has time to worry about it?*

Perhaps representing what some agnostics view as a proper course of action, Cyril Connolly said, "We must select the illusion that appeals to our temperament and embrace it with passion, if we want to be happy."[3] What a sad commentary on the lives of so many people in our society. Just select the illusion that fits your temperament and embrace it with all the gusto you can muster in the pursuit of happiness. Perhaps that's the best an agnostic can do.

The god of the humanist

The humanistic worldview springs from evolutionary origins. This view draws the conclusion that we are the center of the universe and are the controllers of our own destiny. Being the more highly evolved form of our monkey relatives, we are involved in a meaningless process that just happened to begin long, long ago. There is no design, no purpose, and no Designer.

The apostle Paul identified the similar viewpoint of some people in his day and said of them, "Professing to be wise, they became fools, and exchanged the glory of the incorruptible God for an image in the form of corruptible man and of birds and four-footed animals and crawling creatures" (Romans 1:22–23). Paul warned Timothy about the fascination with human knowledge that would come in the last days, and said that it would result in men ultimately focussing on themselves.

Even though they hold to a form of religion, it's devoid of power and reality (2 Timothy 3:2, 5, 7).

Morris, in his book *True Success*, writes, "Knowledge is power, and as the prominent television producer Norman Lear once pointed out to me, self knowledge is the greatest source of personal power on this earth."[4] Lear declares that the ultimate power is understanding self and building life on this knowledge. That is the hope of the humanist.

The atheist says there is no God. The agnostic believes that you cannot know if God exists. The humanist declares that being human is as close to God as one gets.

The gods of the New Age

Been to your local bookstore lately? You'll find whole sections devoted to a belief system called *New Age*. When the apostle Paul wrote to the believers in the city of Colossae, he warned against giving heed to certain individuals who were causing problems in the church. His description also fits those who follow New Age philosophy today: "delighting in self-abasement and the worship of the angels, taking his stand on visions he has seen, inflated without cause by his fleshly mind" (Colossians 2:18; see also Jude 4, 8, and 18–19). New Age really isn't so new after all.

New Age beliefs are simply recycled Eastern religion. It tells us God is everywhere, including in all of us. We are to recreate the god-image within us through advanced learning and mystical spiritual experiences. Remember the television program where Shirley MacLaine stood on a beach saying, "I am god, I am god"? She says god is in all of us and everything is god and god is everywhere. We're all evolving into god. To the person who has embraced this age-old position, we are our own gods.

Contemporary author and motivational speaker, Deepak Chopra, puts a new face on this old approach. His fast-selling inspirational books, audiotapes, and his lectures have paved fresh inroads into American society for neo-Hinduism and

Transcendental Meditation. He teaches that "we must nurture the seeds of divinity within us. In reality, we are divinity in disguise—and the gods and goddesses in embryo that are contained within us seek to be materialized."[5]

Such ideas represent the efforts of those who are striving for something they can't reach. Perhaps in response, someone once said, "In the beginning God created man, and ever since then, man has been trying to return the favor." MacLaine, Chopra, and other New-Agers have chosen how they will spend their time according to their particular belief system. The age-old pantheism of the New Age movement—all is god and god is all—is an inadequate foundation for a truly integrated life.

The god of organized religion

Much of organized religion offers the belief that, *Yes, there is a God and I must find Him.* All religions, with the exception of historic, biblical Christianity, are man's attempt to find God.

The religious person believes that there are two ways to find God in order to bridge the great gulf between His amazing majesty and man's hopeless futility. One way is to reduce God so He can be held in one's hands, or shaped by human fingers, or somehow contained in a little box. Then the religious seeker has supposedly "found God." Of course that is what the apostle Paul was refuting when he said that God is not reducible to a form, or something that you make (Acts 17:29). Trying to reduce God that way is called *idolatry.*

Another way a religious person may attempt to approach God is through personal merit. This requires being morally good enough, plus following rules and regulations with an emphasis on one's deeds. The hope is that if I can excel in learning a catechism, sacrifice my time to engage in religious service, and try my best to attain to a high moral code, I will be in good standing (and maybe even achieve relationship) with God. Paul again warns us against the futility of keeping days and feasts in order to connect with God (Colossians 2:16–23). Building your own bridge to God doesn't work, yet this is how some people answer the question "Who is God?"

The God of the Christian

The apostle Paul wrote a letter to the Christians in the city of Ephesus that tells us some important things about the God who saved them even though they were sinners.

> You were dead in your trespasses and sins, in which you formerly walked according to the course of this world, according to the prince of the power of the air, of the spirit that is now working in the sons of disobedience. Among them we too all formerly lived in the lusts of our flesh, indulging the desires of the flesh and of the mind, and were by nature children of wrath, even as the rest.
>
> But God, being rich in mercy, because of His great love with which He loved us, even when we were dead in our transgressions, made us alive together with Christ (by grace you have been saved), and raised us up with Him, and seated us with Him in the heavenly places, in Christ Jesus, in order that in the ages to come He might show the surpassing riches of His grace in kindness toward us in Christ Jesus.
>
> For by grace you have been saved through faith; and that not of yourselves, it is the gift of God; not as a result of works, that no one should boast. For we are His workmanship, created in Christ Jesus for good works, which God prepared beforehand, that we should walk in them.
>
> (Ephesians 2:1–10)

Yes, there is a God and it's not that I must find Him. He found me!

We have been reconciled to our Creator through Jesus Christ. He is sovereign, great, holy, and powerful; yet full of grace. He is the God who is actively involved in my life and is shaping my future into a plan that has significance. Tim

Stafford, in his book, *Knowing the Face of God*, says, "If the Bible carries one repeated message about God, it is that He wants to be known." This is solid, foundational truth!

Paul talked about this God when he addressed the philosophers in Athens, where people had constructed an altar to an unknown god, and were actively shaping idols and worshiping in ignorance (Acts 17:22–31). He explained the truth to them: "The God who made the world and all things in it, since He is Lord of heaven and earth, does not dwell in temples made with hands; neither is He served by human hands, as though He needed anything, since He Himself gives to all life and breath and all things . . ." (verses 24–25). Paul told them that God is sovereign and mighty. Man can't build a bridge long enough or a tower high enough, wide enough or strong enough to reach Him.

God doesn't need anything since He Himself gives life and breath to all things. Paul said, "He made from one, every nation of mankind to live on all the face of the earth, having determined their appointed times, and the boundaries of their habitation" (verse 26). Paul told them that God is actively involved in creation, then went on to say that He is not far from each of us. That's the God of the Christian.

These are the various major worldviews from which one chooses the foundation for his or her life. There is the atheist, the agnostic, the humanist, the New Ager, and the many efforts of religious persons to bridge the gap between humanity and deity. Then there is the God who can find you, if He hasn't already. He is the living and true God who is actively involved in the affairs of humanity. These are the options, and from one of these starting points, you make your life-management decisions.

The famous and often controversial theologian, Paul Tillich, argued that God is "the ground of being," and is the "ultimate reality" of one's foundation.[6] Whatever one thinks of Tillich's views, this concept seems very relevant. If we want to have a stable foundation, then we all must find a "ground of being" and an "ultimate reality" upon which to build our lives.

Choose carefully. Your identity, purpose, values, priorities, goals, and the way you use your time will all stand or fall on this foundation. Choosing self, doubt, or some smorgasbord of your own imagination will produce devastating consequences, both temporal and eternal. When the true God is your foundation, look forward to the adventure of living an integrated life.

The effect of a personal theology

Let's briefly look at some illustrations of how an encounter with the one true God changed people's lives.

Old Testament encounters

First there is Noah (Genesis 6:1–9:29), who made a crucial decision that affected the course of his life. He encountered the living God in the midst of a society that was headed in the wrong direction. Noah found grace with God, and from that moment on he literally went against the tide. When the judgment waters of the Flood came, Noah's obedience was proved right—he had spent his time constructively and had built an ark to rise above the Deluge. His whole sense of identity, purpose, and mission changed when he came to terms with God.

Next, there's Abraham (Genesis 12:1–17:21), who was known as Abram before his encounters with God. His name and identity were completely changed after experiencing God. His values and direction in life were also changed. God promised that through Abraham's lineage all the families of the earth would be blessed. His descendants would be more numerous than the stars. Try penciling into your appointment book all that goes into becoming a father at a very old age, with a wife who is also chronologically challenged. Even Abraham and his ninety-year-old bride found that one difficult to comprehend, that is, until it happened. His entire life and ours have been different because of what Abraham discovered about who God is and what He does in keeping with His promises.

Then there's Jacob (Genesis 28:10–22; 32:3–32) who, in a dream, saw a ladder set on the earth with its top reaching to heaven, and the angels of God were ascending and descending on it. During his second divine encounter, Jacob wrestled with God all night long; from that moment on he had a new name, a new mission, and a new reality.

And then there's Moses (Exodus 3:1–4, 9) who saw the burning bush and came away from that experience with a new identity and purpose for living. The list could go on and on.

New Testament encounters

Three of the Gospels introduce us to Andrew and Peter (Matthew 4:18–20; Mark 1:16–18; Luke 5:1–11), who were involved in their daily routine as fishermen when Jesus walked by and said, "Follow me." Now, what would you do if a stranger walked by and said those words? Most people would reply that they had appointments to keep, lunch to eat, a wife or husband at home, a career to develop, or places to go.

Peter and Andrew knew that they had responsibilities and opportunities. Why would they stop everything to follow Jesus? The minute they saw Jesus, they encountered God, and suddenly they had a greater reality upon which to build their lives.

Their understanding of who God is—their answer to this question—changed their identity, mission, values, and priorities in life. This resulted in changed goals, which in turn revolutionized how they used their time. All because they had encountered God.

We've already noted the outstanding example of Paul, the apostle. He was on the road to Damascus to apprehend fugitive Christians with their execution in mind. On that journey, he encountered Jesus Christ. Because of this experience his name (formerly "Saul"), his purpose, and his direction in life was changed. All because his theology—his view of God—came face-to-face with truth.

We could write page after page about the biblical characters whose lives were transformed once they had encountered God and believed Him. We could also tell story after story about people in more recent times who were revolutionized once they came to terms with God's claims and character. However, the living illustration of how a clear and compelling encounter with God can change a life needs to be the one each of us observes in the mirror every day.

Prepare for interference

So how do you implement a view of God in your life? Where does a person start? An important first step is recognizing possible misconceptions, and clearing out the interference that blocks our view of God.

Recently we had cable television activated at our house. Out of necessity, we have many channels blocked because the content is not welcome within the walls of our home. For a period of time, we could not get clear reception on several of the remaining channels. Some would show nothing but snow; others were barely discernible; still others came in with minimal interference; yet some were crystal clear.

I finally was motivated enough to call for repairs when I couldn't watch ABC's *Monday Night Football*. (You can tell where my priorities are!) After a house call the serviceman informed us that a loose connection going into the TV set was causing the interference.

As I look back on that incident, it would have been foolish to be angry with ABC when I couldn't get the game. The problem was *not* with the national network nor their broadcast signal. It wasn't even a fault of the cable company's transmission capabilities. My loose connection was the problem.

Our failure to view and understand God correctly is like that loose connection. He is sending us all the signals necessary for us to get a clear picture of who He is. However, sometimes we become angry at Him due to the interference we often experience that often results in confusion, doubt, and/or frustration. Yet, the problem is not with the sender. It's with the receiver, and our distorted reception produces misperceptions.

Evaluating and erasing the old tapes

In his outstanding book, *God in the Dark,* Os Guinness speaks of two obstacles that hinder our understanding of God. The first is "pre-Christian presuppositions" that remain after we have come to faith. We are "born and bred" in an incredibly secular and philosophically eclectic culture. Old assumptions may never have been tested against the truth of who God really is. These confusing ideas can cause considerable interference in our reception.

These presuppositions can also be a result of growing up in homes where unhealthy and imperfect views of God go unchallenged. Our view of God is affected by our home environment and the authority figures in them. Even those who grew up in a Christian home are not immune from inaccurate and distorted ideas about God. Many people have been raised, or are being raised, in grossly dysfunctional families. Hyperauthoritarianism, performance-based acceptance, inconsistency, lying, moral unfaithfulness, and abusive anger are just a few of the negative personal experiences that bias the formulation of invalid presuppositions. Like interference on our TV screens, these influences distort the picture we receive about who God really is.

There is a sense in which our hearts and minds are like a spiritual VCR camera that is constantly recording. We come into the world hungry for truth and spiritually receptive. We record a lot of messages in our receiving center. Eventually, these tapes are filled with all kinds of images and ideas—some true, some false. It is important to assess the content of those tapes, where the messages came from, and the credibility of the sources. Our erroneous ideas about God must be recognized, erased, and replaced with the truth that will set us free (John 8:31–32).

The tape is still rolling

Guinness identifies "alien presuppositions" as a second hindrance that we construct even after committing ourselves to Christ. It's common for people today to build a "God-view" based on ideas borrowed from a variety of world religions, mixed with a measure of personal preference.

One ingredient that often appears in the mix is *relativism.* This worldview denies the existence of absolute truth. Guinness explains the dilemma of holding a mixed up view of God and says, "If God really were like our picture of Him, then doubt would be valid. But it is our picture of God, not God, that is at fault, and the doubt is fueled solely by misunderstanding. Sometimes when I listen to people who say they have lost their faith, I am far less surprised than they expect. If their view of God is what they say, then it is only surprising that they did not reject it much earlier."

Your theology needs to be based on the truth, not on patterns set by Dad, Mom, grandparents, or teachers—no matter how clear or distorted. Truth is being sent your way right now. Ask God to help you tune it in and tune out the interference of this tainted world system. We must deal with the interference on our screen and call for truth's repair to clear it for us—as soon as possible.

Listen to the strong and clear signal God is sending. He has provided every means necessary for us to know Him truly, and to know Him well. He earnestly wants us to have Him as the firm foundation upon which we build our lives. That is why we have the written historical record of God's self-disclosure—the Bible. This supernatural book tells us that it is inspired by God so that we may know Him, not just know about Him. It is His love letter to us, telling us all that we need to know about having a relationship with Him.

Recognizing God's signal

In the Bible, God enables us to have a substantial and accurate understanding of His character. He describes Himself, for our benefit, in *anthropomorphic* terms. These terms connote images associated with our humanness. For example, He is identified as a king, lord, judge, lawgiver, potter, father, mother, lover, healer, teacher, shepherd, provider, protector, servant, and friend. The Bible also describes the eyes, mind, heart, arm, feet, and hand of the Lord. We are able to understand and are familiar with these human roles and descriptions of various parts of the human body.

The Bible also presents Him in *non-anthropomorphic* terms. These terms connote images that are non-human, but they are things that we recognize immediately. We read about God as a shield, fortress, rock, fire, light, eagle, lion, bear, mother hen, cloud, wind, breath, and spirit.

Additionally, we see God's *relational dimensions*. He is loving, merciful, good, truthful, wise, gracious, forgiving, tender, long-suffering, humble, just, wise, and righteous. While remaining absolutely perfect, He is also, at times, wrathful and jealous.

Finally, the *transcendent realities* of God are the attributes that we cannot really relate to, but can begin to comprehend because of His gracious written revelation to us—the Bible. God is: all-powerful, all-knowing, all-present, perfect in holiness, eternal, unchanging, infinite, sovereign, self-existent, entirely self-sufficient, and ultimately beyond comprehensive or exhaustive comprehension. Are you beginning to get a clear picture?

But God, in loving determination, went further than all of these biblical descriptions of the truth. Not only do we have written revelation, but we also have a living example. Because God so wants us to know Him, He entered into our world so that He could be seen, heard, and touched. His feet walked the streets of Jerusalem. Drops of His blood fell on the ground beneath the cross. The apostle John said, "In the beginning was the Word, and the Word was with God, and the Word was God" (John 1:1). John also said that we have seen His glory, "glory as of the only begotten from the Father . . . . who is in the bosom of the Father, He has explained Him" (John 1:14, 18). Jesus is God's explanation of Himself. So, if you want to have a firm foundation of truth upon which to base your life, study Jesus Christ.

Jesus is God's explanation of Himself.

Along with the living truth (Jesus) and the written truth (the Bible), God has sent the indwelling truth—the Spirit of God—to live within those who believe the truth (John 14:26; 16:4b–15). If I wanted my children to really understand the truth in life, I would likely do three things: try to explain the truth, endeavor to demonstrate the truth by the way I live my life, and hire a personal tutor to assure that they continue learning the truth. God, in His perfection, has provided a personal tutor who wants to live in us into all the truth (John 16:13). The Holy Spirit helps us to understand who God is and teaches us to apply the truth in our lives. This happens only as you commit yourself to the lordship of Jesus Christ as revealed in the written truth of God. Unless God truly lives within you, the basis for making life's decisions will forever remain a broken pillar of facts and ideas. It will never be an integrated, solid foundation of truth.

God wants you to know Him more than you even want to know Him. When you commit yourself to follow Christ, by His resident power, knowledge, and wisdom, He will teach you about Himself. As you spend time with Him and study about Him, you will grow in your love and understanding of Him. This is how to develop a firm foundation of truth for your life.

Recording the right signal every day

Now we are going to get very practical. We have reached a point where we will begin to consolidate our thoughts on paper. We need to take these ideas and write a "Personal Theology Statement." I'm not talking about a long doctoral dissertation. What I have in mind is just writing down a series of life-changing truths about God, based upon His Word.

Let me make two quick disclaimers. First is the obvious fact that God cannot be reduced to words or human thoughts, let alone a written statement on a piece of paper. This is simply a place to begin. Second, writing your thoughts is a lifetime exercise that you'll edit and revise as you grow in understanding God's truth. Nevertheless, this is a starting point for highlighting and specifying the realities that touch your life at the deepest level.

Many of us, when it really comes down to it, live like practical atheists. Our view of God doesn't change our lives. I believe that nothing is dynamic until it is specific. That's why it's a good practice to write down your view of God. As one man said, "Thoughts disentangle themselves as they pass through the lips and over the fingertips." Author William Faulkner said it this way, "I never know what I think about something until I read what I've written on it."[7]

The Israelites, the people to whom God gave His laws and commandments, were commanded to bind passages from God's word on their hands and foreheads, to write them on their doorposts, as well as to teach His word to their children (Deuteronomy 6:4–9) Why? Because the word of God must be worked into the fabric of your life.

Here is an example of what I have written down, which I constantly review. What a difference it makes! Perhaps it will give you some ideas.

My God is the CREATOR, so all of life has divine design and spiritual purpose.

My God is absolutely SOVEREIGN. Even when life seems out of control, He is firmly in charge.

My God is completely GOOD, even when circumstances and people seem bad.

My God is always JUST, even when life feels unfair.

My God is unconditional in His LOVE. Nothing that happens and nothing I do can cause Him to love me any more or any less.

My God is full of GRACE. He will forgive and strengthen my weaknesses and enable me to do the same for others.

My God is HOLY. His absolute moral purity is untainted by this sinful world—and so should it be in me.

My God is ALL-KNOWING. There is no motive, thought, or detail of my life about which He is unaware.

My God is ALL-POWERFUL. There is no personal struggle or life-problem beyond His capability of handling it with ease.

My God is ALL-PRESENT. There is no secret place in my world apart from His comforting peace and holy presence.

My God is completely WISE. He has all the answers to any question or issue that perplexes me.

My God is the LORD JESUS CHRIST. He is the perfect and radiant picture of God. He is the model and master of my life.

My God lives in me by the HOLY SPIRIT. He is my constant companion performing a perfect and powerful ministry of encouragement, guidance, and teaching.

As you can see, it really helps to be specific. Write out your view of God, then write what this view means to you. Hopefully, you can live and pray it as your view is shaped to correspond to what the Bible teaches about God. Writing down what you learn about God as you read the Bible influence your life decisions—and ultimately your management of time.

Review is important

As the prophet Jeremiah said, "Thy words were found and I ate them, and Thy words became for me a joy and the delight of my heart . . ." (Jeremiah 15:16). God's Word should mean so much to us that as we ingest it, the truth becomes a part of who we are. It is meant to be a genuine delight to our hearts. His word becomes a joy in our life because we know who we are in relation to Him.

Over the years I have been in the process of writing out my answers to all seven questions discussed in this book. They are in my time-planning system, and I review them virtually every day of my life now. Eventually, I also recorded my answers on a cassette tape and listen to them on a regular basis. What I have written is not a substitute nor an improvement on Scripture, but I want to get up every morning knowing who God is, who I am in Him, knowing why I am here, what really matters, what I'm going to do, how I'm going to do it, and when it will be done. I want all of my decisions and actions to be based on the truth of God's Word, not on emotional subjectivity nor the clamoring noise of the world.

Tim Stafford, in his book, *Knowing the Face of God*, says, "We drag out of bed in the morning, force our eyes to focus on the words of Scripture, mumble words into space, and get moving toward work, where God may not even be mentioned, where He certainly does not appear . . . . One day rolls over into the next, and we cannot spend forever asking speculative questions about the whereabouts of God."[8] Most of us tend to detach the reality of God from the day-to-day grind that we all face.

The Bible talks about renewing our minds according to the truth. Why? Because the world is always trying to conform us to its skewed way of thinking about God, the meaning of life, and ourselves. Daily renewal can begin with reviewing the answers we have written.

Benefits of a clear theology

Thinking is hard work. My kids remind me of this every week when we talk about the importance of their schooling. They attend what is called in California, a *fundamental school*. These institutions don't have all the bells and whistles of other schools, but they have a very high standard for learning the fundamentals. It's tough work for students who choose this course of study. But someday, my kids will be glad they studied hard. It's just a little challenging to convince them of the benefits of rigorous learning right now.

Thinking about your theology is kind of like attending a fundamental school. It's a call for hard work on the basics. We are talking about mastering the basic building blocks of life. Yet the benefits are absolutely amazing. Let's look at the impact of a theology that is tested, tried, and true. We need these reminders about why we should be practical and consistent in renewing our minds. Here are six positive benefits of having a clear view of who God is.

Strength for life's stresses

One benefit of having a trustworthy theology is strength for life's stresses. Centuries ago, in the third year of Cyrus, king of

Persia, a message was revealed to the prophet Daniel that described the amazing turmoil of the pagan world while Israel remained captive in Persia. The angelic messenger said to Daniel, "the people who know their God will display strength" (Daniel 11:32). The idea is that, in spite of all the appeasement and influence of the world, people who truly know God and know Him well, are going to display strength.

Yes, life is full of stresses and distractions. But our main source of stress is that we depend too much on things that change. For instance, you may have lost a job in the last month or two. Or perhaps you've lost a loved one who just doesn't want to see you anymore. Maybe it's a wife who has been in a bad mood three days straight, or a husband who is too wrapped up in the NCAA finals.

Recently, a member of our congregation sat in my office. She was broken and confused, and her shattered heart was full of questions. After twenty years of a rocky marriage, her husband had decided that he didn't love her anymore. A former sweetheart from high school had recaptured his heart and, for him, divorce was the only reasonable option. Their three adolescent daughters waited on the sidelines, wounded and watching as this marriage unraveled.

This deeply troubled mother sat before me and asked, "Can I somehow get my husband back?" She wanted to know how she could raise the girls, handle legal costs, and deal with all of the other problems that arise during times like these. I tried my best to help her understand that, while these questions seemed urgent, they were not the most important ones to be asking. The more important question was, "Who is God?" What did God want to reveal to her about Himself in all of this? Then, how could that reality become a bedrock of support for her while her world was experiencing an emotional earthquake?

Even though life is full of stresses and distractions, the things upon which you can always stand and build your life are the rock-solid promises of God. When we do this, we will be strong because of His strength.

Courage for life's challenges

Another advantage for those who have a tested, tried, and true theology is courage for life's challenges. The angelic messenger who spoke to Daniel also said that the people who know their God "will take action" (Daniel 11:32). He is talking about people who will not only demonstrate strength, but also will rise to the challenge and overcome. When you make some clear distinctions about who God is, write them down, and integrate them into your life, you will be not only strong, but also courageous, regardless of life's stresses.

Peace in life's trials

The third benefit of a trustworthy theology is an amazing, indescribable peace, no matter what happens. God says to us what the psalmist wrote: "Cease striving and know that I am God" (Psalm 46:10). The impact of this verse can be phenomenal. Some versions translate the first couple of words as "be still." This idea can also be translated, "let go" or "relax." When we know God, were are able to do so.

How many people say, "Oh, my problem; do you know how bad my problem is?" Or "How tough things are," or "How poorly people are treating me," or "How low my checking account balance is," or whatever the issue is. The real question that should be asked and answered has to do with how a person is viewing God.

Why cease striving? Because "I am God" says the Lord. Isaiah 26:3 says, "The steadfast of mind Thou wilt keep in perfect peace, because he trusts in Thee." God has promised. He is the God of peace. He doesn't just give peace, He *is* our peace (Ephesians 2:14). That doesn't change because this is who He is. If you will keep your mind stayed on Him, you too will experience peace. When you know who God is, you can have quiet rest in the midst of life's trials.

Companionship for life's journey

Next comes the benefit of divine companionship for life's journey. After Nebuchadnezzar king of Babylon had taken captive the king of Judah, his officials, as well as craftsmen and smiths from Jerusalem, God told the prophet Jeremiah what He would do for captives of Judah. He said, "I will give them a heart to know Me, for I am the LORD; and they will be My people, and I will be their God" (Jeremiah 24:7). You see, God puts into our hearts the capacity to know Him, but not just for the sake of knowledge. It's for a dynamic relationship. One where divine companionship becomes the norm in your life. He will be with you through the easy times and the hard.

Most of us are familiar with the poem, *Footprints*. It's about a person's past trials, and the bewilderment of seeing only one set of footprints in the sand, even though Jesus had promised to walk beside the person and be there during those hard times. In the poem, this was Jesus' response: "My precious, precious child, I love you and would never leave you. During your times of trial and suffering, when you see only one set of footprints, it was then that I carried you."

When you don't know God, you are a slave to whatever false god you create.

He was there as the person's divine companion. God's presence becomes the assurance of those who know Him, who have a theology that helps them understand that no matter what happens, relationally or circumstantially, God is in the midst of it all.

Freedom in life's choices

Another benefit is freedom in life's choices. The apostle Paul wrote to the churches of Galatia and said, "When you did not know God, you were slaves to those which by nature are no gods" (Galatians 4:8). These are the gods who have eyes but can't see; ears but don't hear. In other words, no power, no response. People who worship false gods go unheard, and remain enslaved, powerless and, alone.

When you don't know God, you are a slave to whatever false god you create, whether it's you, the created being, or an idol. But when you are committed to the true and living God, you come to know the truth and the truth makes you free.

For several years, our church has hosted prayer summits. These three-and-a-half day getaways are intense times with God for the groups that meet together. With no tightly structured agenda, we spend hours far from the hustle and bustle of life, reading the Bible, singing praises, and offering worship.

During the summit, people respond to God in natural and sincere ways. For the first time, many come to truly comprehend God's unconditional love and acceptance. This enables them to share weaknesses, in freedom and security, and to ask others for their support in prayer. Some are confronted with God's holiness and deal with areas of long-overlooked sin with unprecedented honesty and humility. Then there are those who, in light of the forgiveness and grace of God, confess their sins and find new resolve to work toward substantial healing of broken relationships.

The woman who sat in my office, questioning what to do about her fractured marriage, returned just days ago from a women's prayer summit. She went, in the midst of her pain, to get to the bedrock of a personal theology. She returned revolutionized by a fresh infusion of "intimate theology." Shortly afterward, her husband left a message on my voice mail and said,

"Pastor, we're ready to meet with you to rebuild our home on the foundation of God's truth. We want to put things back together." He too has found a bedrock of truth. For them, the foundation of having a solid theology has made all the difference.

Hundreds of people have been dramatically affected by these prayer summits. I have seen firsthand the transforming power that God releases when people come to terms with Him as they gain a deep and accurate understanding of His character. The variety and depth of these stories is profound, and there are too many of them to tell now. But people are set free to see themselves as they really are—and to be secure and content in the identity they have in Christ. They are infused with a new sense of purpose. They rearrange priorities and establish worthwhile goals. How people choose to spend the precious commodity of their time changes when the interference is cleared up so they can receive a strong signal and get a clear picture of God!

Assurance in life's uncertainties

Although we could go on about the advantages of having a clearly defined theology, we will finish with the benefit of assurance in life's uncertainties. Prior to when Judah was taken into captivity to Babylon, then God said, "Let not a wise man boast of his wisdom, and let not the mighty man boast of his might, let not a rich man boast of his riches; but let him who boasts boast of this, that he understands and knows Me, that I am the LORD who exercises lovingkindness, justice, and righteousness on earth; for I delight in these things" (Jeremiah 9:23–24).

Not only does the Lord delight when you boast in Him—in your knowledge of Him—but notice that the reason for boasting is because "he understands and knows Me." We are not just talking about a cognitive understanding, but of an intimate knowledge of a living Person. When this is true in your life, you live with the assurance of God's daily blessing and provision.

What's the wisdom expressed here? Don't take pride in your wisdom or your strength. All of these change. If you're going to rest your assurance on one thing in life—one thing that never changes—rest on understanding and knowing God. It's been said that he who is enslaved to the compass is free to sail the seas. This is the assurance known by those whose compass is set on the character of God.

The most important question in life is not about a career, where to live, how big the paycheck is, or even about health. The most important question is "Who is God?" An answer that is biblical, accurate, and powerful will make all the difference.

A certain commercial that captured my attention the first time I saw it illustrates what we've been discussing in this chapter. The setting of the scene was the downtown streets of a large city late at night. Homemade signs were posted in various places pointing the way to a plate of tacos on the sidewalk. Standing near his "bait" was the cute Taco Bell chihuahua. In his mouth was a rope tied to a stick holding up a box with which he hoped to catch his prey. In the darkness of the night he called out, "Here, Lizard, Lizard."

Soon the pounding footsteps of a very large creature could be heard. The ground began to shake. There it was—the approaching figure of Godzilla. At the sight of the oversized lizard, the little dog promptly dropped his rope and in apparent shock uttered, "Uh-oh! I think I need a bigger box!"

Like the little canine, we are on a quest to find something that may prove bigger than we expect. In our case, it is God. But our little box is too small for the discovery. The purpose of this chapter has been to challenge preconceived ideas of God by digging deeper in the "foxhole" of a working theology. If your idea of God has been challenged, your heart may be crying out, "Uh-oh. I think I need a bigger box." You're right, we do.

Truly, the God of the universe makes Godzilla look like a flea by comparison. Yet, because of His lovingkindness He is revealing Himself to us. He wants to be found, more than we even want to find Him. So let's allow our box to expand as our theological foundation develops and settles. Then we'll be ready to build a more integrated life as we renew our minds with a view of God that's bigger than what any box could ever contain.

A personal guide to developing your theology

Use the following chart to begin developing your clarification of God's character. This will become a helpful tool in writing your personal theology. The summaries of God's attributes in Appendix 1 will be of help to you. Use the answers in column 3 in conjunction with Question 2 ("Who am I?"). Note the examples.

God is . . .	Therefore, He is . . .	Therefore, I am . . .
Good	Always committed to my best interests. Working in a positive way even when things feel negative.	Genuinely optimistic and victorious; grateful in all things, never a "victim." Content in all situations.
Just	Always fair in His dealings; the judge who will make everything right, now or later.	At peace and trusting Him at all times. Able to endure unfair treatment without retaliation or bitterness.

Question 2

"Who am I?"

*Help, I am being held prisoner
by my heredity and environment!*
Dennis Allen[1]

*A truly healthy view of self amounts to
seeing yourself as God sees you.
No More. No less.*

My first recollection of an identity crisis dates back to my childhood and relates to a children's book entitled *Are You My Mother?* In this story, a baby bird hatched while its mother was away. This placed the little fledgling right into the middle of its own identity crisis.

Wandering all around his immediate world, this fearful feathered one asked, "Are you my mother?" He questioned a dog, a swan, a heavy-machinery crane, a bulldozer, and everything else in his path. Each answer failed to provide the information needed in his search for self-identity. Happily, at the end of the tale, he finds his mother and all is well.

In some sense we all can understand the crisis of the little bird. Even though we have learned to ask the questions of *Where do I belong?* and *Who am I?* in a more sophisticated manner, our crises are just as real.

Counselor Larry Crabb says, "The basic personal need of each person is to regard himself as a worthwhile human being."[2] William Glasser confirms the need for personal worth when he says, "Everyone aspires to have a happy, successful, and pleasurable belief in himself."[3]

Only when we understand who God is are we able to truly discover who we are.

Sooner or later, we all face certain foundational questions: What is the basis of my self-identity? How do I come to regard myself as worthwhile? Am I like the little bird, trying to discover my identity in relation to a parent or someone in my immediate surroundings? Or can something, or Someone, more reliable than me help me discover who I am? Most importantly, will this discovery result in security?

I believe that only when we understand who God is are we able to truly discover who we are. In establishing this theological foundation, we saw that atheists base their lives on the assumption that God does not exist. An agnostic wonders whether or not God exists, but reasons that if He does, He probably can't be known. The humanist asserts that he himself is God, while the New Ager says, "We are all gods."

When we believe that God doesn't exist or that "I am God," then the foundation is self or some other humanly constructed idol. This is a shaky base upon which to build one's life.

We looked at the religionist who says, "Yes, God exists, and I must somehow find Him." Finally, there is the Christian who says, "Yes, there is a God, but He found me."

Perhaps it seems strange to think of self-identity as being so pivotal to personal well-being and life-management, but over the years I have found this basic hypothesis to be true:

We all spend our lives either searching for, attempting to prove, or confidently expressing our identity.

Roles versus reality

In 1976, I arrived in Lynchburg, Virginia, and entered a new world—college life. I came with eager anticipation since my older brother, Dennis, was a professor and staff pastor in the megachurch associated with the school. He was well-known and respected around campus. This was easy for me to accept since he was not only my brother, but also one of my heroes.

Although the surroundings were unfamiliar to me, one thing was certain—I was "Dennis Henderson's little brother." Even though no one knew my name, they could identify me because of my brother. This gave me a sense of dignity and security. I felt significant because I was associated with one of the school's "bigwigs."

The following years brought many opportunities to this "little brother." I became a member of the official singing team that traveled with the chancellor and sang on the nationally televised church services. Among other things I was elected student body president during both my junior and senior years.

In the span of three years, I was no longer the "little brother." In fact, the roles reversed and my hero became "Daniel Henderson's big brother." We were both really amused by this role reversal; but more so, we were both reminded of the shakiness of personal identity when based on human opinions or achievements.

The basis of identity

Some of us are still trying to figure out who we really are. Others have chosen a certain identity and are investing a great amount of time in establishing it before the watching world. They invest their energy into proving their personal worth, acceptability, and value. In our own way, we all tend to find security in our identity, although at times in some pretty strange ways. Our significance may spring from our family name, personal achievements, physical appearance, or social connections. These are all shaky foundations, and in a matter of time or with a change of circumstance, our sense of significance can fade very quickly.

Wise Christians base their identity on the reliable basis of biblical truth about God. This rock-solid foundation can shape a healthy self-image in a powerful and lasting way. Furthermore, we can experience a truly transformed existence based on new life found in Jesus Christ. In Him, we have a secure foundation that lasts forever. By renewing our minds in the truth of His Word, and His declarations of who we are in Him, we can weather the role reversals of life with peace and endurance.

It's been said, "You are what you eat!" And someone has claimed, "You are what you wear!" The truth is, you are what you are. So the question is: "What are you?" More importantly, "Who are you?" This issue of identity is not simple. Its complexity encompasses five different dimensions of identity: *eternal, experiential, external, essential, and effective.* Each of these helps us to understand who we are.

Our eternal identity

First, let's consider the eternal dimension of identity. This is the fundamental issue for man since he is a spiritual creature by God's design. In Genesis 1:27 the Bible specifically and distinctively describes the creation of man: "God created man in His own image, in the image of God He created him; male and female He created them."

God breathed the breath of life into man, and man became a living soul. From the beginning, we have been spiritual beings, distinct from trees, animals, plants, or any other segment of God's creation.

Man was created with a spiritual capacity. God has set eternity in our hearts (Ecclesiastes 3:11). Deep within we are aware of something beyond our physical existence—we possess a spiritual sensitivity to that which is eternal.

Our unique function in God's plan

The current trend in our country toward spiritual things reminds us that there is an unseen realm that coexists with the physical creation. Our neighbors, while living in time and in space, are searching for spiritual experiences. We see it in Hollywood with major films and television programs featuring Buddhism, spiritual encounters with aliens, and people from all walks of life "touched by an angel."

Genesis 9:6 reminds us that, even after Adam and Eve rebelled, human beings still bear the unique image of God, although marred, as it were, and in need of renewal. What does this mean? It has to do with the holistic makeup of humankind—his mind, will, and emotion.

Our minds have the capacity to use logic and reason like God reasons. Unlike animals with their instinctive behavior, human beings are endowed with volition—the ability to choose. Mankind has the distinctive faculty of emotion.

Our family has a copy of the classic animated Disney video, *Jungle Book*. We have watched it numerous times over the years. It has been delightful to watch Baloo, the jovial bear, while feeling trepidation when the huge snake Kaa slithers across the screen, hissing threats. Laughter fills our family room as Louie, the king of the orangutans, dances and prances. And then there's Bagheera, the sleek black panther, who gives friendly advice to the boy Mowgli on his journey back to the Man Village.

Over the years we've also enjoyed the lovable and winsome Winnie the Pooh with his laughable friend Eeyore. I also remember Bullwinkle, Scooby-Doo, Bugs Bunny, and my childhood favorite—Huckleberry Hound. Or, how about those trees from the Wizard of Oz? Not only did they talk, they even threw apples at Dorothy and company, in retaliation for having been "picked-on."

But the life portrayed in *Jungle Book*, *Looney Toons*, or *The Wizard of Oz* is, for the most part, not true to life. Animals don't talk, dance, or interact in the same way humans do. They don't write books, graduate from college, organize political parties, attend church, or celebrate birthdays. They don't build police stations, elementary schools, or monuments. Nor do they promote conferences on spirituality.

Certainly, if animators and producers can imagine animals having these capacities, one would think God could have created singing bears, mischievous rabbits, and angry trees. And, yes, He could have. But He did not. God made mankind with a unique eternal awareness distinguishing us from the rest of creation. We were custom made according to His special design.

Spiritual on purpose

Along with being created with this dimensional likeness of God, we have been created for a purpose—the ultimate purpose of experiencing affirmative spiritual relationship with Him. Ephesians 1:4–6 clarifies this when it describes God's purposeful design in the lives of those who have come to know Him: "He chose us in Him before the foundation of the world, that we should be holy and blameless before Him. In love He predestined us to adoption as sons through Jesus Christ to Himself, according to the kind intention of His will, to the praise of the glory of His grace, which He freely bestowed on us in the Beloved." This potential allows us to interact meaningfully with God, and with each other. Being able to relate beyond the physical will continue for eternity, each person is an eternal soul.

During my seminary days in central Virginia, a group of Christian graduate students asked if I would conduct a series of campus seminars at the University of Virginia. Several weeks prior to this series, I met with some of them for orientation and prayer. Afterward, one of the students invited me to tour the medical school's cadaver room. I went for the experience, though not enthusiastically.

What I saw in that massive room will never leave me.

As we entered, a pungent smell of formaldehyde filled my nostrils. Before me were scores of work tables occupied by the remains of people who had recently been active, living human beings. My gut knotted in response to the detailed inspection of the "specimens." Some were still essentially intact. Most were not.

Later, during the long drive home, my mind was filled with deep spiritual and emotional reflection. In those moments, physical existence seemed so very futile and fragile. Without eternal life (John 17:3), life's journey appeared ultimately hopeless and without meaning. I thought about the people who live as if our brief journey on earth were nothing more than physical appearance and pleasure. In that regard, they have nothing to look forward to but a six-foot hole, a crematorium, or a cadaver room. What a shame to go through this life ignoring the spiritual dimension put within us by divine design.

God is most glorified in us when we are most alive in Him. A clear, biblical, and life-applicable answer to the question *Who am I?* breathes energy into all that follows. The good news is that I can be "alive" with a clear sense of identity, purpose, and direction in life when the reality of my relationship with God is the foundation for all of life's choices. Otherwise, life is a cadaver.

Because we are spiritual beings, we will continue to exist beyond the grave. Every one of us faces an eternal destiny—a destiny determined by our theological foundation. It is either in heaven with our loving Creator or eternal separation from Him who granted us the ability to choose freely.

Either way, we all face an eternal existence. This is our eternal identity, one uniquely true to all mankind.

Our experiential identity

Remember the illustration in the previous chapter about the videotape running in our hearts and minds from birth? We talked about the fact that our ideas of God are sometimes misshaped by the input we receive from the temporal world around us. The same concept is true of our conclusions about ourselves. From day one, the environment in which we live and the people with whom we share it have been wielding strong influence on our self-perception. Unfortunately, at times the environment is spiritually toxic. The people who live in it are morally flawed because of sin.

We're all trying to find ourselves while, at the same time, keeping our heads above the surface of moral quicksand. At an interpersonal level, it is like a group of completely lost people trying to find north without a compass. Granted, some of this input is balanced and healthy. However, much of it is biased and hurtful.

Ephesians 2:1–3 describes our spiritually toxic environment and depraved internal world and says, "You were dead in your trespasses and sins, in which you formerly walked according to the course of this world, according to the prince of the power of the air, of the spirit that is now working in the sons of disobedience. Among them we too all formerly lived in the lusts of our flesh, indulging the desires of the flesh and of the mind, and were by nature children of wrath, even as the rest." We are living as fallen creatures in a fallen system. Like the opening quote of this chapter, we feel we are being held as prisoners— and we are, until the truth sets us free.

Adam and Eve pollute the environment

The experiential dimension of life includes "Who am I?" in light of this fallen and deceptive world. You see, God created man in His image to enjoy perfect fellowship with Him and with each other. But Adam and Eve decided to live independently, to make their own choices, devoid of God's wisdom. In doing so, they rejected this relationship.

So, how did their decision affect you and me? The Bible says that because Adam sinned, and because we all come from the same ancestral stock, each one of us has been born into our fallen state. It's found in Romans 5:12, 16: "Just as through one man sin entered into the world, and death through sin, and so death spread to all men, because all sinned . . . . judgment arose from one transgression resulting in condemnation."

When Adam and Eve separated themselves from God, several things happened. First of all, they expressed insecurity (Genesis 3:7–10). Before this, they had lived in perfect fellowship and harmony. They didn't need any type of covering because they had nothing to hide.

As soon as they chose independence from God, they knew they were naked. That's how the Fall affected you and me. We became like God, knowing good and evil (Genesis 3:22), and this introduced our first parents, and us, to self-consciousness, self-centeredness, and insecurity. We, as they, became externally focused.

We aren't sinners only because we sin. We sin because we are, by virtue of the Fall, sinners. A marred likeness of God's image remains, but our spiritual lightbulb is out. Even though we have a dim understanding that the light of truth exists, we continue to live in spiritual darkness, having lost the ability to spiritually relate to God and to each other.

Our ancestral parents also realized that they were alienated. For the first time in their lives, they hid from God. When He sought them they began to accuse and blame. Guilt led them ultimately to blame God. It's the same old story. Adam blamed Eve, Eve blamed the serpent, and the serpent didn't have a leg to stand on.

God said their willful independence would result in painful childbirth, sweat from working hard, and death. From that time forward, frustration, blame, alienation, and insecurity have been a part of the reality of nature and existence.

I believe that the strategy of Satan used against Adam and Eve is the same one he uses against you and me. He wants us to misunderstand God, to doubt His word and character, and then to keep us in constant confusion about who we are. This internal confusion results in conflict, insecurity, and alienation in our relationships. If he does nothing more than this, he's won the battle. We will live defeated lives.

Is this fact a reality for you? It is for me, because this world has had many years to shape my identity from the outside in. This world taught me that if I didn't perform in a certain way, I may reap the anger of a parent or friend. It gave me the false idea that my acceptability depended on conforming to other people's expectations. My life-management was guided by such information. The humor in this impossible situation is that some of these people, and their standards, were as skewed as mine.

Ironically, the people who set standards of perfection for us are usually unable to meet the criteria themselves. Still, we continually attempt to meet the unreasonable expectations of imperfect parents, imperfect spouses, imperfect employers, and our imperfect selves. All the while, our fallen world continues to successfully bombard us with these ideas.

Input! Input!

I remember watching a video called *Short Circuit*. It's about a government-designed robot that escapes from its inventors. In seeking to interact with a vast new world of sights, sounds, and people, it developed an independent intelligence and personality. In its quest for understanding it constantly exclaimed, "Input! Input! Robot Five needs input!"

That's how we live. As babies we yell, "Input! Input!" When we grow older, Mom or Dad may say, "A good child gets A's and B's, not C's and D's." Many of us, for whatever reason, may have grown up as overachievers in our experiential identity. Because the input gathered from a variety of sources during childhood is so influential, I constantly have to renew my mind and realize that I don't have to perform, achieve, or be liked in order to be valuable.

Beethoven, in his early adult years, had a teacher who told him that as a composer, he was hopeless. Edison's teacher told him that he was so stupid he would never learn anything. Albert Einstein was flunked by his math instructor. Walt Disney received walking papers from his first job at a newspaper. The editor said he had no capacity for creativity. Input! Input!

How about you? Did you grow up with any of this imperfect input? If so, it has probably resulted in a life of constant comparison, of always overvaluing other people and undervaluing yourself—or vice-versa. Either tendency is a skewed way to live. It's the result of faulty data received from a fallen and deceived world that is affected by sin.

Speaking of sin, the definition of this politically incorrect word has also been skewed. The term doesn't have so much to do with the issue of whether you "smoke or chew, or go with girls who do." It has to do with a willfulness of heart.

Author and theology professor, David Needham, says that "sin is the expression of an individual's response to the issue of meaning apart from the life of God."[4] Sin is an attempt to find meaning independent of God. We turn to outside input and grow up with a faulty sense of experiential identity based upon external input received from imperfect people. Thus, most of us take our cues from people, instead of from God, and that input jeopardizes the fulfillment of our God-given potential.

Our external identity

When was the last time you stood in front of a mirror and took a good look at the image it reflects? You may have said, "I look pretty good in this new dress!" Or maybe you thought, *How did I get so old so fast?* Perhaps you secretly admitted, "I don't like myself." The problem is that your outward appearance doesn't reflect who you really are. It is only part of the package—like it or not.

This third dimension of "Who am I?" has to do with external physical features. Physical appearance is not easily changed, apart from extensive surgical procedures. But don't we try?

People with straight hair tend to want curly, while those with curly want straight. Some without any just want hair. Thin people desire more shape, heavy ones want less. Those who are light-skinned want to be darker, and others with darker tones want lighter skin. There are even some women who want to be men, as well as men who want to be women. We are so confused!

If only we understood that a good and sovereign God made each one of us unique, we wouldn't be so dissatisfied with our external identity.

The issue here is the difference between image and identity. We live in an image-oriented society. Those who look good seem to get the promising jobs, the rich spouses, and the cover stories in the entertainment magazines. But a sense of identity and personal security too dependent on image is a house of cards. When life gets tough and crows' feet appear around your eyes, self-worth can come tumbling down.

A poignant scene from the movie, *Deep Impact*, showed a team of young astronauts preparing to embark on a mission to destroy an asteroid heading toward earth. They gathered at a social event and were being photographed by various members of the press. One veteran astronaut was looking on and in his private conversation made the comment, "They are not scared of dying. They're just scared of looking bad on TV." To some degree, his comment describes the way our society elevates image over substance.

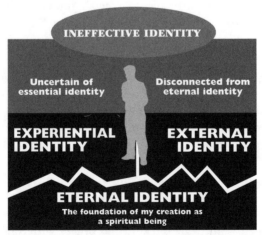

The Bible teaches that even before we were born, God knew everything about us. He made us the way we are, and He doesn't make junk. There is divine design in the color of our hair, the features of our face, and the measure of our stature (see Psalm 139).

But what about someone who was born maimed at birth? If his or her identity is based on physical appearance or in comparison to others, life is going to be tough. If people's opinion about one's "attractiveness quotient" is vital to one's well-being, trouble and heartbreak are inevitable. Certainly any tragedy that damages our physical appearance is unfortunate. But for those who have a strong foundation, physical defects don't uproot who they are. Their physical problems don't cause the house to crumble.

My friend Ken is one of the most inspiring people in my life. Back in the early 1980s, Ken was in dental school in the Chicago area. He and his fiancée were stopped at a light on an exit ramp next to a tanker truck filled with gasoline. Another large truck appeared in the rearview mirror. Suddenly, the approaching semi slammed into the back of the tanker. Ken and his fiancée were immediately engulfed in flames. She was killed. He had severe, life-threatening burns over most of his body. His very life was "touch and go" for weeks. The pain and heartbreak were unbearable.

After months of excruciating treatments, multiple skin grafts, cosmetic surgeries, and ongoing therapy to improve his blood circulation, Ken started life over again. On the outside, he looked completely different. To some his appearance was probably repulsive. But on the inside, Ken Campbell was still Ken Campbell—only stronger and better. Thanks to the power of God's Word and the enduring love of family and friends, he is more in touch with himself and his Lord than ever.

ABC's *Wide World of Sports* featured Ken's story. Not only did Ken recover and become an avid runner, he competed in the Iron Man Triathlon in Hawaii. Today he has a successful dental practice in Sacramento. He is also a respected leader in local politics. He is an avid student of God's Word. He is a model church member and ministry leader. Several years ago, Ken married a lovely Christian woman. He works hard on his rural ranch and is raising two beautiful daughters.

I love and respect Ken. He is one of my dearest friends. Over the years I have learned that Ken is not his skin. Ken is the man who is within. Most people who know Ken don't even notice his extraordinarily scarred face and hands. We just know him as one of the finest individuals we've ever met.

Double trouble

For many, this issue of external identity is too intricately woven with our sense of real identity. A tragedy like Ken's would be the doorway to unending despair. When we place too much importance on outward appearance and fail to understand the inner identity, life seems fragile and lacks true integrity. When we add in the abundance of skewed data received in life, we have double trouble.

The foundation of our identity is the fact that God has created us in His image as fundamentally spiritual beings. However, those who do not have an authentic relationship with God do not have this foundation. For them, identity is based on and is limited to experiential and external factors.

Anyone who doesn't have Christ in his or her life has yet another problem. Such a person's identity is based on the external and experiential aspects of life—both of which can be superficial and deceiving. Deep down inside, a person who has not been made spiritually alive struggles with his identity. This individual isn't sure how to get a grip on life. The result is often a constant identity crisis. So, how does one get past this frustration? The answer is found in the dimension of essential identity.

Our essential identity

So far, we have explored the first three dimensions of identity (eternal, experiential, external). These dimensions are characteristics common to everyone born into this world. But the dimensions of *essential* and *effective* identity are unique to those who are spiritually born again.

With spiritual birth comes a whole new dimension of identity. In fact, this new dimension supersedes all the others.

Essential identity features "Who am I?" in light of the Person and work of Jesus Christ.

Essential identity features "Who am I?" in light of the Person and work of Jesus Christ. And the answer is found in 2 Corinthians 5:17: "If any man is in Christ, he is a new creature; the old things passed away; behold, new things have come."

We are told that the power of Christ makes us new people. Colossians 3:3 confirms this: "You have died and your life is hidden with Christ in God." The old creature is one who has taken all its cues from this world of condemnation and sin; one who was traded in for an essentially new person.

How you see yourself versus how God sees you

The distinction between our self-perception and God's view of us can be illustrated by creating a fictitious person. Let's make him be a middle-aged male, married, and willing to answer the following questions:
Q. "Do you consider yourself passive or aggressive?"
A. "Passive."

Q. "Tall or short?"

A. "Tall."

Q. "What color is your hair?"

A. "Dark brown."

Q. "What is your profession?"

A. "I'm a business administrator."

Q. "Are you married?

A. "Yes."

Q: "Do you have children?"

A. "Yes, we have a boy and a girl."

Q. "What is your ethnic background?"

A. "Northern European."

Q. "Now, when you were growing up, did your parents ever say that you were a certain kind of person—aside from being a perfect child?"

A. "I was a brat."

That's who this fictitious man is externally and experientially. He is tall, passive, middle-aged, married, a father, and a business administrator with dark brown hair. He is Northern European, and a brat.

Now the Bible says that when a person such as this man came to Christ, he became a new creature. In the book of Ephesians we are told many things about him. For starters, he is a saint (1:1). Once he realizes this, not only will the world see him in a new way, but he will see the world and himself differently.

We are also told that this person is "blessed" and was "chosen by God before the foundation of the world" (1:3–4). If someone who is always wise, correct, truthful—and omniscient—said that about you, would it make a difference in your life?

Not only is this individual in Christ blessed and chosen by God, he is also "holy," "blameless," and "sealed in Him with the Holy Spirit" (1:4, 13). Now, he may not feel holy, but God says he is. His wife may not agree that he's blameless, but God says he is. He may not feel secure, but that doesn't change the fact that, in Christ, he is most assured.

And this is only the beginning. We read that he is God's "workmanship"and has been "created in Christ Jesus for good works" (2:10). You see, he is a new creature in Christ. Knowing this should make a substantial difference in a person's life.

How many of us, who have been reconciled to God, know the reality of once being dead, but now being fully alive? The old person, who took skewed cues from all the wrong places, is now a fundamentally new person who receives truth revealed by God as his input.

In the back of this book you will find a comprehensive list of the New Testament passages that give you God's truths about who you are in Christ (Appendix 2). Make it a habit to read through this regularly as a powerful reminder of your new identity in Him.

Addition or transformation?

When you came to Christ, your whole identity changed. You are not just a sinner saved by grace. There's not an old nature and a new nature destined to fight for power and control. No, the Bible says you have been born again; you are a completely new person, a saint who happens to sin because of your vehicle of vulnerability—the flesh.

One seminar speaker, when discussing this topic, said that a believer is basically a spirit critter in an earth suit.[5] Isn't that descriptive? We're not sinners who received an addition of good things from God. No, it's not an addition. It is a transformation. We've gone from being sinners to being saints!

But you say, "I don't think of myself that way." That's the problem! It's really not an issue of human opinion. It's an issue of reality, an issue of what God says. A believer must stand in the truth of God's Word and live accordingly. David Needham, author of *Birthright*, explains it this way:

> A Christian is not simply a person who gets forgiveness,
> who gets to go to heaven, who gets the Holy Spirit, who

gets a new nature. . . . . *a Christian is a person who has become someone he was not before.* A Christian, in terms of his deepest identity, is a *saint*, a child born of God, a divine masterpiece, a child of light, a citizen of heaven. Not only *positionally* (true in the mind of God but not true in actuality here on earth), not only *judicially* (a matter of God's moral bookkeeping), but *actually*. Becoming a Christian is not just getting something, no matter how wonderful that something may be. *It is becoming someone* (emphasis added).[6]

Because you are in Christ, God sees you as He sees His Son. Your old person died, was buried, and has risen as a new creature. How can that be? It's because, for God, there is no limitation of time. He chose you before the foundation of the world: so when Christ died on the cross, you died; when He was buried, you were buried; when He arose, you arose. And now, with Him, you are seated in the heavenlies. This is spiritual reality.

A new man—on assignment

But why are we left here in this earth suit? Why do we continue to struggle? Because the Lord has a mission for each one of us, an assignment to tell others about God's offer of new life in Christ.

The idea of *mission* bleeds to the next question: "Why am I here?" As we will see, purpose in life (or the lack thereof) springs from our sense of identity. As "saints," we are left on this earth as new people for an important purpose.

Think about the options. If our earthly purpose were simply to worship, God would not have left us here after He transformed us since our worship will be perfect in heaven. Acquiring knowledge of spiritual things is a vital function of our new life—but it's not the ultimate goal. Knowledge will be perfect in heaven. Why stay here? Fellowship is a wonderful experience—but it's not the ultimate aim. Our relationships will be perfect in heaven. God would not leave us here with the potential of conflict and misunderstanding if this were His primary earthly design for our lives. These are important elements of the new life, but all of them will be experienced in heaven more perfectly than on earth. If these things were the immediate purpose for a new person, He would have "beamed us up" after He brought us to Himself.

There is one thing we cannot do in heaven that we must do here. We must live as new creatures in such a compelling way that when spiritually dead people hear and believe the good news of Jesus Christ, they will be made alive. We must bring our friends, relatives, associates, and neighbors to understand God's offer of essential identity in Christ.

To be frank, this assignment brings opposition. We're told about the conflict being waged in heavenly places (Ephesians 6:12). It's no surprise that we have an enemy who goes about like a roaring lion, approaching us through our vehicles of vulnerability (1 Peter 5:8–9). Perhaps it would help us remember the reality of this invisible warfare if instead of greeting each other with, "Hello, how are you?" we asked, "Hello, how goes the battle?" We fight a winning battle when we renew our minds in the truth of our new identity in Christ (see John 16:33).

Our effective identity

I'll never forget the night I sat in a Seattle hotel enjoying a few moments of personal conversation with Bill Bright, founder of Campus Crusade for Christ. After a special event where we had shared the platform, I asked his advice about some ministry struggles I was encountering. Among many other words of wisdom, he made this statement: "Every soul is precious, but not every Christian is strategic."

It's one thing to know how precious I am to God. He loves and values me forever. It is another thing, however, to be submitted to Him so that His power might turn my new person into a life of supernatural impact.

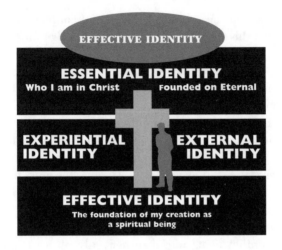

Here is where we come to "who I can be" in the light of the design and enabling of God's grace. This is the issue of our effective identity. Great insight on this is found in Ephesians 2:10 where we read that He designed and enabled us for effectiveness. That word, *effectiveness*, is a life-management word. Effectiveness is the result of integrated living.

Discovering your Spiritual DNA

To help bring the goal of effectiveness to remembrance, I use the acronym: "S-DNA," which stands for our "Spiritual DNA." Just as we all have a unique physical code (DNA), so God has made every Christian unique in how he or she is wired for effective service. The "S-DNA" represents spiritual gifts, desires of the heart, natural talents, and aptitudes. Seen as a whole, these form a distinct and effective identity.[7]

First, there are the *spiritual gifts*. The Bible says, "Now there are varieties of gifts. . . . to each one is given the manifestation of the Spirit for the common good" (1 Corinthians 12:4, 7).

God has given each believer at least one gift with which to make an effective difference. These gifts involve the ability to minister with supernatural ability and impact in serving others to the glory of God. So many Christians have no idea how their spiritual giftedness works. They fail to understand what they are and why they're given. Numerous books and study guides are available on this topic, so we need not be confused. The fullness of effective identity is not possible until this area of spiritual gifts is understood.

Next, we have been given unique *desires of the heart:* our motives and interests. "It is God who works in you both to *will* and to do for His good pleasure" (Philippians 2:13 NKJV, emphasis added). God works through our desires to direct and motivate us according to His purposes. For instance, God has shaped my heart to be passionate about certain areas of ministry. Preaching, catalyzing renewal through prayer, working with leaders, and connecting with strategic global missions truly motivates me.

But if you were to talk with individuals on our church staff, one of them would say that his heart is with youth ministry. This person, so to speak, eats, sleeps, drinks, and breathes young people. That's his heart, his passion. It's what motivates him and yet is distinct from his giftedness. Another staff member is motivated to equip people, to mobilize them to serve in practical and powerful ways. Another has a heart for children.

Each of us has a unique heart, and that's part of God's design for effectiveness in our identity with Him.

When it comes to *natural talents*, Exodus 36:1 provides an illustration: "Every skillful person in whom the LORD has put skill and understanding to know how to perform all the work in the construction of the sanctuary, shall perform in accordance with all that the LORD has commanded."

We all have God-given abilities. Some people are good in science. God can use this. Others are good in music, and God brings forth effectiveness from this talent. However, some of us aren't very talented in this area. In fact, I was recently sitting in front of a prison singer. You know what a prison singer is, don't you? It's someone who's always behind a few bars and is never able to find the right key. We may not have obvious musical talent, but that's all right. Instead, we may be good with words or have natural ability in mechanics, carpentry, art, sports, organizing, or cooking. These natural abilities are part of our effective identity.

Then there's *aptitude*. Linked to our individual personalities, this word describes our unique learning styles and approaches to life. Over the years, through various assessments and experiences, I have learned that I am a conceptual thinker—an idea guy. I am an extrovert. My leadership style is inspirational and entrepreneurial. I am motivated to influence others. Knowing this helps me to recognize how and when God might want to use my unique design to His glory and others' good. This uniqueness within each person is, indeed, a vehicle for God. As Paul wrote in 1 Corinthians 12:6, "There are varieties of effects, but the same God who works all things in all persons."

Differences in aptitude are easy to see in group dynamics. In an office, some workers are most productive in an organized environment where everything is in place. Others are comfortable with a little creative confusion. One person likes routine, another seeks variety.

When approaching a situation, some of us work through it with our feelings first. Others think things through very logically and methodically. It's the same with extroverts and introverts, leaders and followers. We all approach life in a variety of ways, yet God brings effectiveness out of our differences.

Our aptitudes are shaped and revealed by personality and life experience. Our educational, cultural, and spiritual experiences can all affect our approach to life. "All things work together for good to those who love God, to those who are the called according to His purpose" (Romans 8:28 NKJV).

So these are four dimensions that shape our effective identity. Many base their personal identity on what sociologists, psychologists, parents, friends, co-workers, or teachers say about them. But for me, I would rather base my identity on what God says, because that is truth.

Twentieth Century Fox's version of the mysterious and famous story of Anastasia, the exiled daughter of the czar of Russia, reminds us that having an identity and living out that identity are not synonymous. She was a woman of royal birth and earthly notoriety. Yet, throughout most of her life she never knew it. Nor did anyone else. She spent most of her years never having understood nor having experienced her true identity.

Four keys to experiencing your identity

Fullness of identity begins with *receiving Jesus Christ* as your Savior and Lord. Just as all died in Adam, all can be made alive in Christ (1 Corinthians 15:22). "The free gift is not like the transgression. For if by the transgression of the one the many died, much more did the grace of God and the gift by the grace of the one Man, Jesus Christ, abound to the many. . . . For if by the transgression of the one, death reigned through the one, much more those who receive the abundance of grace and of the gift of righteousness will reign in life through the One, Jesus Christ" (Romans 5:15, 17).

Although death entered into human experience through Adam, all can be born again in Christ. Being born a second time creates identity—it transforms a victim into a victor. With a new understanding of who you are, wrath, rejection, pain, antagonism, and negativity can be reshaped by the truth that you accept in Christ. You will know that in truth, you are loved, you belong, and you are complete.

The truth is that you carry the worth of God's Son. He cared so much for you that Jesus came and gave His life in order to provide you with a totally new one. In Christ, that is essentially who you are. In Him is a thoroughly new, valued you.

After receiving Christ comes the *renouncement of the deceptions* offered by this imperfect world. The enemy of your soul is using this fallen system in an attempt to consistently deceive you about the truth of who you are. If he can immobilize you at this level, he has immobilized you for the rest of your life.

To renounce something is to declare it untruthful. Imperfect data received from imperfect people needs to be declared for what it is. Now, that doesn't mean all of this imperfect data is incorrect, because there is wisdom in counsel. We're talking about identity, not actions. Many times we don't live like children of God. That's when loving correction is needed (Hebrews 12:4–11).

What should be renounced are statements such as these: "Well, you're not worthy, because you don't compare to him [or her]," or "You are less than worthwhile because you didn't perform in a certain way." Recognize this as part of the deceptive condemnation of the system. You need to speak the truth and say, "I may not attain to the standard that he [or she] did, but I still have great worth because of Christ; I am accepted, because of Christ; my security is not based on imperfect input, but on what He says about me."

I'm reminded of the story about little eight-year-old Johnny. Early one morning he came running into the kitchen and said, "Mommy, I just measured myself and I'm six-feet tall!"

His mother expressed surprise and said, "Six-feet tall? How did you figure that?"

Johnny raised up to his best height and responded, "I made my own measuring stick!"

Many of us measure ourselves by our own measuring stick, or with one provided by the people around us. Then we wonder why we often fall short. It's time to use an accurate measuring device—the one provided by God.

Renouncing deception leads to *recounting the truth about yourself.* Galatians 6:14–15 says, "May it never be that I should boast, except in the cross of our Lord Jesus Christ, through which the world has been crucified to me, and I to the world. For neither is circumcision anything, nor uncircumcision, but a new creation."

Begin to discover what God says about you. Paul knew that he was crucified to this world and the world to him. The world, for him as for us, is no longer the basis for our identity or significance. Colossians 3:10 makes this clear by stating that we are to "put on the new self who is being renewed to a true knowledge according to the image of the One who created him." The key phrase is renewal to a "true knowledge."

Even after teaching the Ephesian Christians many monumental truths about their true identity, Paul understood the need to remind them again to "be renewed in the spirit of your mind, and put on the new self" (Ephesians 4:23–24).

A story is told in *Lutheran Digest* about a man named Harvey, who was being interviewed on his 110th birthday. The reporter wanted to know how he accounted for his longevity.

"You might call me a health nut," Harvey replied. "I never smoked. I never drank. I was always in bed and sound asleep by ten o'clock. And I've always walked three miles a day, rain or shine."

"But," said the reporter, "I had an uncle who followed that exact routine and died when he was sixty-two. How come it didn't work for him?"

"All I can say," replied Harvey, "is that he didn't keep it up long enough."

Consistent *renewal of the mind* is required. "As he thinks within himself, so he is" (Proverbs 23:7). So, what were your thoughts about yourself today? Were they shaped by truth or error? Were your thoughts oriented around what people said or what God has said?

A 1991 survey of men in the ministry taken by Fuller Institute of Church Growth showed that fifty percent of those interviewed felt totally inadequate. Seven out of 10 said they have lower self-esteem now than they did when entering the ministry. The issue of identity is a battle that requires a continual renewal of our thinking.

The term *renew* means "to make new again." We are told to renew our minds in Romans 12:1–2:

> I urge you therefore, brethren, by the mercies of God, to present your bodies a living and holy sacrifice, acceptable to God, which is your spiritual service of worship. And do not be conformed to this world, but be transformed by the renewing of your mind, that you may prove what the will of God is, that which is good and acceptable and perfect.

Transformation comes through renewing our minds according to God's truth. More important than putting on fresh clothes every day is the need to be renewed and reclothed with our new identity in Christ.

Making renewal real—every day

Just because you've "heard this all before" doesn't mean that you're living out your identity in Christ. There is no value in merely hearing. Truth applied and translated into action is what matters. Renewed thinking about who we are in Christ needs to be constant and consistent; it is the key to our wholeness and the accomplishment of His will.

I've written a simple "Identity Statement" and I review it daily. While not exhaustive, it highlights the basic truths of who I am in the light of God's reality:

"I, Daniel D. Henderson, am a new creature in Jesus Christ—a completely loved, fully accepted and totally empowered child of the most loving, most high, most holy God. I have been created by His amazing grace for a life full of good works and God's glory through Christ, my Lord."

The statement above expresses my essential identity. It overrides my experiential and external identity. It shows the fulfillment of my eternal identity as fundamentally spiritual—created and designed by God to know Him. It is a foundation for my effective identity, since this is the essence of who I am, based on the truth of God's Word and His work in my life.

Soaring with the eagles

The story is told about an eagle that was found by a farmer and raised among the barnyard ducks, chickens, and turkeys. It ate chicken food, drank out of the same container, and even behaved like a chicken.

One day a naturalist was visiting the farmer. He said, "That bird is an eagle, not a chicken."

"Well," replied the owner, "it may measure fifteen feet from wing tip to wing tip, but I raised it to be a chicken, so it no longer is an eagle."

"No," said the visitor, "it is still an eagle. It has the heart of an eagle and has been created to soar heavenward."

The farmer remained adamant. So, they agreed to a test where the visitor would have three days to make the majestic bird fly.

On the first day, even after much coaxing and encouragement, the eagle was more interested in jumping down onto the ground and joining the barnyard fowl for scattered grain. On day two, although reminded that it had the destiny and heart of an eagle, the regal bird chose dirt, barnyard fowl, and chicken food.

On the third day, early in the morning, the naturalist took the eagle to a high mountain. Raising it up to survey the golden landscape and glistening peaks, the naturalist said, "You are an eagle. You belong high above, freely soaring through this expansive sky. Stretch your wings and fly."

The eagle looked over the valley below and hesitated. Taking the bird's head, the naturalist turned it directly toward the sun. An age-old quiver surged through the feathers and with a mighty shriek, the bird flapped its powerful wings and soared toward the beckoning blue heavens.

Victory comes from understanding who God is, and then understanding who you are in Christ. A confident expression of one's identity is found in knowing Christ—a secure knowing that is based on truth. This is the only sure foundation for a life of lasting integrity.

A personal guide to confidently expressing your identity

Step one: my eternal identity

We are all created in the image of God with an everlasting soul and a body of flesh. God desires to make us spiritually alive through an authentic relationship with Him through His Son, Jesus Christ. However, the Bible says we were born in sin. The result is spiritual death and judgment (Romans 3:9–18; Ephesians 2:1–3).

For personal reflection:

Do you know that you have been made alive by entering into a relationship with God through Christ? If so, take a moment to describe when and how that happened. Write your testimony below. (After you've finished, meditate on the "before and after" description in Ephesians 2:1–10. Take some time to thank God for the difference He's made through the power of salvation to make you a completely new person.)

If you are not confident that you have been made alive by entering into a relationship with God through Christ, turn to Ephesians 2:1–10. See God's description of your current spiritual condition in verses 1–3. Consider what He is able to do as seen in verses 4–10. Now turn to John 1:12–13. Ask God to do a work of grace in your heart today. Pray that He will open your eyes to your need for Him. He will enable you to turn from sin, which separates you from His life, and to receive Christ as Lord of your life. By His power, He can make you alive spiritually and give you the assurance of eternal life in His name (see John 10:27–28; 17:3). If you desire to make this decision right now, write out your prayer of commitment to Christ below.

Step two: my experiential identity

During your developmental years, what factors in the world around you formed concepts that have been destructive to your sense of security and well-being? Make a list of these things (derogatory names, crisis experiences, put-downs, hurtful criticisms):

In what ways have these formed a shaky foundation for your life?

Take time now to commit any hurt, disappointment, or confusion to the Lord. Admit to God any erroneous ideas you've adopted about Him. Confess any sinful behavior that is connected to these sinful views. Admit your need for a renewed mind and perspective toward yourself. Write your prayer here:

Step three: my external identity
List the aspects of your external appearance that you often do not appreciate:

Read Psalm 139:13–17. Confess to God your willingness to trust the wisdom of His handiwork in making you. Thank Him for the way He has fashioned your external identity. Ask Him to take any weaknesses and use them to glorify Himself by His grace (2 Corinthians 12:9–10). Write that prayer here:

List the aspects of your external appearance that you most appreciate:

Now, recognize that these, too, are gifts from God's good hand. Remind yourself that He gave you these for His glory, not yours. Review 1 Samuel 16:7, Romans 12:1–2; and 1 Corinthians 6:19–20. Write down a prayer that reflects these verses as it relates to your external person.

Step four: my essential identity

Review the list (Appendix 2) of "Who I am in Christ." Thank God that every one of these things is true—because He said so. Take time to list the truths that especially counteract the negative inputs of your past or motivate you toward the future.

Now, begin to craft a biblical "Identity Statement" that incorporates some of these truths and expresses who you really are.

Step five: my effective identity

Begin now to think about your S-DNA (Spiritual DNA).

Spiritual gifts

Review Romans 12:6–8; 1 Corinthians 12:1–31; and 1 Peter 4:7–11. List the gifts that seem to interest you or the ones that you've seen active in your life:

Write down the ways in which you have served the Lord in the church and have seen a supernatural result in people's lives:

Desires of the heart

Write down the areas of involvement or service that you tend to gravitate toward and which, when you are involved, are very rewarding:

Natural talents

Write down some of your natural abilities, which can be used to honor God as He empowers them.

Aptitudes (temperament, learning, and communication styles):

Write down some of your personality strengths and weaknesses (ask the opinion of some friends or co-workers who will be honest with you).

Strengths:

Weaknesses:

How do you usually learn most effectively (by seeing examples, by listening, by asking questions, by reading, by writing)?

How do you best function when working with a group of people?

Now review the various answers you gave to the above questions (re: S-DNA). Try to write a summary paragraph based on these observations. In doing so, finish this sentence:

I am most fulfilled and effective in serving God when I . . . .

Question 3

"Why am I here?"

The great tragedy in life is not death,
but life without reason.
Myles Munroe[1]

The great use of one's life is to spend it on something that will
outlast it; for the value of life is computed not by its duration,
but by its donation.
William James[2]

The purposes of a man's heart are like deep waters,
but a man of understanding draws them out.
Proverbs 20:5 (NIV)

Many of us spend our lives chasing after things that the world convinces us we must have in order to be significant. We never discover who God is, who we are, or why we're here. An advertisement for a popular Hollywood movie summed up the world's message in the following words: "From the dawn of time man has struggled for just four things: Food. Safety. Someone to love. And a pair of shoes that fit."

Yet this is why Jesus came: to set you free from the drumbeat of this world, free from expectations of other people, and freedom to know Him and know who you are in Him. Whether or not your shoes fit is secondary.

A light-hearted story has been told about a young seminarian eager to find opportunities to speak. One afternoon he had the occasion to address a fairly large group of patients in a mental hospital. He chose the subject of "purpose" as the focus of his message. He began his sermon with the question, "Why are we here?" For dramatic purposes, he asked the question several times allowing for a pregnant pause between each inquiry. After the third time one fellow at the back became frustrated with the speaker's inability to find an answer to his own question. He stood to his feet and shouted, "Young man, we're all here—because we ain't all there."

Until a person knows why he or she is here, that person's life really has no meaning. The fact is that God wants you to live a life of purpose, of significance, a life that is clearly yours because of Him. He offers you an opportunity to live a life that, when it is over, you can look back and know that you lived well.

Set me free and let me live

In his book, *In Pursuit of Purpose*, Myles Munroe tells the story of one young man who apparently experienced such a moment when he stood before the thunderous applause of an excited crowd. The mayor of the city made this announcement: "Ladies and gentlemen, it gives me great pleasure to present, for his distinguished service to his community, the Annual Outstanding Citizen of the Year Award to Dr. Clyde Wilson, Jr."

A well-built, clean-cut young man rose to his feet and walked confidently toward the stage. At the table sat his mother, Emily, and his father, Clyde Wilson, Sr. This was the moment they had been waiting for, the moment to see their son become all they had envisioned for him. As pride filled their hearts, they knew that no one in the room could ever understand their sense of accomplishment, satisfaction, and fulfillment.

You see, Mr. Wilson, Sr., had always dreamed of being a medical doctor. While his son was quite young, the father told him that he would do whatever it took to see that his son reached that goal. Young Clyde's parents labored at many jobs over the years and lived without certain conveniences just to make it possible for their son to attend medical school and complete his internship. This evening all those sacrifices were worthwhile, for Clyde, Jr., now brought honor and respect to his family.

As young Dr. Wilson held the plaque, the crowd rose to their feet. Cameras flashed and shouts of congratulations filled the room. Everyone waited for his response. For a moment he stood erect; then his composure broke. With tears flooding his eyes, the young man pleaded with his parents in a voice that mirrored the despair in his eyes. He said, "Please, Mom and Dad, forgive me. I'm sorry, but I can't go on."

Bewildered and embarrassed, the chairman helped the young doctor off the stage. The crowd stood in questioning shock.

As Clyde and his parents drove home, he attempted to explain his uncontrollable behavior. His words spilled over one another as he tried to describe the last ten years of growing frustration. "Everything I have accomplished and achieved during these years," he said, "has been done to please you and to fulfill your lifelong dreams. I have become what you wanted me to be, but I have never become who I am.

"In spite of all the cars, houses, and other material things I possess, my life is empty. I never wanted to be in the medical profession like you did, Dad. In truth, I hate being a doctor.

"I've always wanted to be a musician," young Clyde continued, "but you and Mom would not allow me to follow my dream. Please understand, I love and respect you deeply and know all you've sacrificed to provide my education. I thank you for it. But tonight I realized that I cannot continue to fulfill your dreams and expectations. I must start fulfilling God's plans for me.

"When I accepted that award tonight, I felt like a hypocrite," he said. "Someone I don't even know earned it, because I don't know myself. I want to come alive, I want to be what I was born to be. Please," he said in desperation, "set me free and let me live."[3]

The young doctor is a living example of making a wise and bold choice, for it's not how long you live, but how meaningfully (purposefully). You're not really ready to live until you know what you want written on your tombstone. If you were to die today, would those who know you be able to say, "This is why [he or she] lived"? Is it clear to you why you are here? When this life comes to an end, will you look back and conclude that you have lived well and significantly?

A meaningful life requires purpose. This is true of groups, societies, churches, families, relationships, and individuals. "History shows," voiced one observer, "that the value of life decreases and the quality of existence diminishes when a generation loses its sense of destiny and purpose."[4]

It's apparent in our world today that people have no idea why they are here, governments don't understand why they exist, and whole nations are lost and floundering. A discerning writer put it this way: "We preserve nature, but kill babies. We build solid houses but cannot construct lasting homes. We are smarter but not wiser; bigger but not stronger. We know more but understand less. We live longer but enjoy life less fully. We write more books but fail to take the time to read them. We go faster but get nowhere. We conquer space but cannot conquer our habits. We protect whales but abuse our children."[5]

Is this the legacy we want to leave? To be smarter, bigger, know more, live longer, write more, go faster, conquer space, and protect whales? Even when it results in being no wiser or stronger, understanding less, enjoying life less fully, having no time to read books, getting nowhere, being unable to conquer bad habits and continuing to abuse our children? Do these goals and results reflect a meaningful purpose?

This highlights the importance of answering the question, *Why am I here?* with a real sense of clarity and in a way that sets you on a course and process that will give your life definition and enduring significance.

The difference between purpose and mission

To know why I exist, why I have been created, is to know God's purpose for my life. To know God's mission for my life is to understand why I am here on earth—right here, right now. Each person's mission (why you are *here)* is important and must be discovered, but that is only the personal and individual aspect. On a broader scale, we are exploring three different aspects of purpose: *eternal, earthly,* and *explicit.*[6] Examination of personal mission is included in the subject of earthly purpose.

Eternal purpose

The Westminster Catechism covers our eternal purpose well: "The chief end of man is to glorify God and to enjoy Him forever." This is the real purpose for our existence. That's why we are here. That's true now and true in eternity.

At a personal level, I have thought about a statement that reflects my understanding of God's eternal purpose for my life. Although it is almost impossible to improve upon the Westminster classic, I have rewritten my own version in this way:

*"I exist to worship, glorify, and enjoy God forever
in an authentic love relationship with Him
through His Son and my Savior, Jesus Christ."*

Earthly purpose

Our earthly purpose is our mission here on earth. As one person put it, "Here is the test to find whether your mission on earth is finished: If you're alive, it isn't."[7] That's fairly simple to understand. Each of us has a mission.

Jesus constantly repeated His mission. His example encourages me to do the same.

As noted in the last chapter, when the Lord saved me and made me His, He could have called me immediately into His presence. Had He done so, my worship would have become more full, my knowledge more complete, and my fellowship with Him would have become perfect. He has reasons for my remaining on earth, however, and it is His desire that I seek to understand this earthly purpose or mission. This is true of every believer who has been reconciled to God through Jesus Christ.

Much has been written about personal mission statements, as seen from a business or corporate point of view. Even so, I believe in the benefit of writing a personal statement, then praying over it and making it a very intimate part of your daily experience. Of course, the benefit depends upon the foundational base of your theology and identity being rooted deeply in God's truth.

An earthly purpose, or mission statement, should remain constant, regardless of age, roles, relationships, setting, location, status, or health. Apart from periodic "wordsmithing" it represents a guidepost for everyday living.

Here is my personal mission statement:

"In response to God's love,
my mission is to fully experience and faithfully express
the love and truth of Jesus Christ
at all times, in every place, and among all people."

As you read through this chapter, I think you'll be motivated to write something similar, but better—because it will be yours.

Explicit purposes

Now we come to the task of discovering our explicit purposes. This happens when we clarify the purpose of our daily roles and relationships. Here's a personal example: What is the purpose of my family? The days can become so routine. We go to work, come home, send the children to school, tidy the house, provide the food. Someday the children will be starting a life of their own. Then we ask, "Why did we do that, Dear? And who are you, and who am I, and why are we married? Do we have, or have we ever had, a clear sense of our mission?"

Although it is possible to get carried away and end up with so many "statements" that you lose the substance, I find the following ideas to be helpful:

Write a statement of eternal purpose that reflects why God made you. Use the Westminster version if it works well for you.

Write a statement reflecting your life's mission. This should describe God's purpose for you on this earth, regardless of age, roles, relationships, location, status, or health.

You may want to create statements of exact purpose for the various roles you fulfill, such as husband, father, wife, mother. What is your purpose in these roles and responsibilities? Make a list of the most important roles you fulfill in life. Next to each one, write a statement that reflects "why" you are fulfilling this role. If you don't know, then it's really important to take time to think about it.

Additionally, the relationships in your life may require you to identify your explicit purpose. These are the "why do *we* exist?" statements. Among these would be family, work, church. Of course, the most important one to begin with is family, but after that should come any important relationships that you have within a group context. Do the larger groups have meaningful mission statements? Do they, and you, know the purpose for their existence? If not, encourage this thinking process.

The "roles and relationships" mission statements obviously will change because these are dynamic dimensions of life. Yet, your earthly purpose will remain fairly intact, while your eternal purpose is a constant forever.

Have you answered the question of why you are doing what you are doing? Do you have a clear sense of purpose for the hours you're investing in that effort? A wise man once said, "Great minds have purposes. Others have wishes." Are you spending your life wishing and wondering, or do you have a God-given purpose that compels you? Until this is clear, you will be confused about what you should be doing with your time, resources, and direction.

Discovering purpose—by the Book

"The LORD has made everything for its own purpose . . ."
(Proverbs 16:4). Guess what? That includes you. Your very
existence is evidence that this generation needs something that
your life contains. One writer explains it this way: "The production of the product does not begin until the purpose for the
product has been established."[8]

If you're in manufacturing, you don't say, "Hey, this looks
interesting. Let's produce some of these, attempt to sell them,
then come up with some reason why we did." Does this make
sense?

Instead a manufacturer says, "There's a need out there. We
want to meet that need, so we're going to design something, produce it, and market it in order to fill this gap." Now I'm not
talking about a Madison Avenue approach where advertising
creates a desire for anything that can be marketed for a profit,
or where the purpose is to make a fast dollar and move on. No,
this manufacturer has a legitimate purpose for production, and
God had a legitimate purpose for creating you. God did not
make a mistake when you entered into this world. He created
you for a reason.

God does have a purpose for your life

He saved you, if you are a Christian, for a purpose. "He
who prepared us for this very purpose is God, who gave to us
the Spirit as a pledge" (2 Corinthians 5:5). His purpose for sav-
ing you is to bring glory to Himself, to make an impact here on
earth. He's put His Spirit in you, not only to reveal that purpose to you, but to enable you to fulfill this purpose. Talk about
a reason for living!

In Acts 13:36 we see that David had a purpose: "David,
after he had served the purpose of God in his own generation,
fell asleep and was laid among his fathers."

Later, in Acts 20:24, we see that Paul was aware of his purpose: "I do not consider my life of any account as dear to myself, in order that I may finish my course, and the ministry which I received from the Lord Jesus, to testify solemnly of the gospel of the grace of God." Notice the word *course*. It's a specific dimension in which he was going to live his life. In 2 Timothy 4:7 he says, "I have fought the good fight, I have finished the course." He knew why he did what he did. And so can you.

Just in case you need one more example, let's observe the most perfect of all. You'll find more than a dozen verses in which Jesus Christ reiterates His purpose. He consistently made sure that people understood "I came [for this purpose . . .]", "The Son of Man has come that . . .", "I have come that . . . ." The Bible consistently reaffirms that Jesus came with a clear sense of mission.

All of His works, miracles, and deeds ultimately flowed from His mission of being born to die in order that we might live. His mission was to shed His blood on the cross that you and I might receive the forgiveness of sins and that He might give eternal life through Himself. He came to give you a reason for existing here on earth and He wants you to know why you are here. He clearly has a purpose for your life.

What a difference a purpose makes

Knowing why you are here will change the way you wake up every morning and the way you live every day.

Do you remember Scrooge in the story, *A Christmas Carol*? Perhaps the most significant event in this wonderful story was the transformation of Mr. Scrooge's perspective on life. After investing his days in greed and self-centered living, he received a vision of how his life might end. He saw himself kneeling before a neglected grave, and after reading the gravestone that bore his name, he was jolted by the realization that there are far more important things in life than the petty focus that had always consumed him. From that moment on, Ebenezer Scrooge devoted his energies toward a new mission in life. For the first time in his life, he understood what it means to celebrate Christmas.

What changed him? He realized he was living for the wrong reason. When he came to terms with the possible outcome of his lifelong course, his whole purpose for living changed. So can yours.

Most of us are more favorable toward change when we can see the benefits. Let me share some of the advantages that a well-defined purpose will make in your life.

Meaningful destination

Let's start with destination. Some people who spent their lives climbing the ladder of success may find that it has been leaning against the wrong wall. To realize that all of one's efforts were for nothing, that it was all meaningless vanity, is a sorry way to finish.

But when we come to Christ and understand who He is, and who we are, we acquire a sense of purpose. We have a destination that matters. The journey proves to be valid.

In 1 Corinthians 9, Paul uses the analogy of athletes who give their all, but end up with a prize that is perishable. In our day it would be like an Olympic runner who sacrifices his or her life in order to run a race that results in a medal and the possibility of being pictured on a cereal box.

Paul says that many run for a perishable prize, but Christians run for a prize that is imperishable. We have a destination that is forever. People who come to terms with Christ's plan and purpose for them have a destination that is meaningful.

Clear direction

Another benefit of purpose is that it provides your journey with clear direction. You have knowledge of the way you should go in order to get to where you're supposed to be. As Paul says, "I run in such a way, as not without aim; as not beating the air" (1 Corinthians 9:26). Just any road won't do for him. He knows his purpose, and his direction.

Today's society is confused and without direction. Young people come out of school not knowing what career to choose or which path to follow. Adults, too, lack focus. The solution ultimately has to do with the question of purpose. When you know that, you know your direction.

Guiding discernment

Knowing your purpose also furnishes the ability to discern. We have an objective basis for making decisions. Should I do this or that, go here or there? Unless you know why you're here, you have no real basis for making the decision.

For example, consider grocery shopping. Supermarkets are full of products that offer hundreds of choices. Wise shoppers bring carefully prepared grocery lists in anticipation of present and future needs. As they go down each aisle they know, based on their budget and food requirements, exactly what is necessary for making wise choices.

Other shoppers rush into the store, grab something that looks good at the time, throw it into the basket with no real sense of price or plan, then check out as quickly as they came in. After they get home, they often realize that they forgot something needed for dinner, or the next day's lunch. Then they have no choice but to drive back to the supermarket. This haphazard behavior typifies their weekly schedules. If they would plan more carefully, they could save both time and money. It's the same with daily time expenditures, as purpose becomes a plan that gives meaning to life's decisions.

Business author Steven Covey, when addressing the topic of decisions, uses the example of the Constitution of the

United States.[9] This is an objective standard by which all other laws are evaluated. It is a document the president agrees to uphold, a criterion by which people are admitted into the citizenship of this country.

That's what purpose becomes for you—a constitution to give you discernment to live wisely and make good choices. It all comes down to purpose. Why are you here?

Powerful determination

Purpose also instills within us the power of determination. I remember hearing Charles Tremendous Jones say, "You can tell someone what to do and they may do it for a little while. But once they believe in why they are doing it, it will take a brick wall to stop them." And philosopher Friedrich Nietsche noted, "He who has a 'why' for which to live, can bear with almost any 'how.'"

It's been said, "a man will give his life for a noble cause, but not for $50,000 a year." Deeply held and consistently applied purpose motivates and fortifies. Jerry Falwell is famous for saying, "You don't determine a man's greatness by his talent or his wealth—as the world does—but by what it takes to discourage him."

So many people just give up. We live discouraged lives because we forget why we're here. If we understand the meaning behind it all, the reason, we can continue. Truly strong and enduring lives are motivated by dynamic purposes. As one person put it, "Nothing contributes so much to tranquilizing the mind as a steady purpose, a point on which the soul may fix its intellectual eye."[10]

Do you have the point of fixation that keeps you calm in the midst of it all? Life is full of change and our society is changing faster and more drastically than ever. We have the spheres of virtual reality, cyber-intimacy, and computerization. It's enough to make a thinking person nervous—unless you know why you are here. If you do, everything around you can change and you will still have a steady sense of purpose.

Perhaps this is what Jesus meant when He promised a peace, not like the kind the world gives, but a transcending sense of well-being. In a similar vein, He told His disciples, "In Me you may have peace. In the world you have tribulation, but take courage; I have overcome the world" (John 16:33). The new life we have by the resident power of His Spirit in us transcends superficial sources of peace. His overcoming purpose raises us above the troubles of life, as we make His purpose our own.

I like to define discouragement as a "temporary loss of perspective." Even though the noise of life screams for our attention, and troubles of life work to derail us, knowing the "why" behind it all keeps circumstances in perspective. Purpose makes sense: "God causes all things to work together for good to those who love God, to those who are called according to His purpose" (Romans 8:28).

Internal delight

Last, but not least, purpose infuses your experience with a sense of delight. That doesn't make the journey easy, just worth it. Life isn't easy. It's not even, as Forrest Gump says, "a box of chocolates."

Now *there's* someone who caught moviegoers' attention. Why did people respond to him in such an overwhelming way? Was it his simplicity, his ups, his downs, his quest for meaning in life? Perhaps deep down inside we all sense that life is like a box of chocolates. That it's just a matter of trying your best to pick the most attractive option in the hope that it's as good inside as it looks on the outside.

Helen Keller said, "Many persons have a wrong idea of what constitutes true happiness. It is not attained through self-gratification, but through fidelity to a worthy purpose." A worthy purpose brings joy.[11]

Jesus knew that. In Hebrews 12 we are told to fix our eyes on Jesus, "the author and perfecter of faith, who for the joy set before Him endured the cross . . . ." Is it possible to endure, with joy, the crosses in life? If the answer is "no," then the issue may be one of purpose.

This is why the early church counted unpleasant circumstances a joy and privilege, even in persecution. They had a reason for existing, and it was not grounded in personal popularity and acceptance. They were driven by a mission, the mission of Jesus in their lives. If that is true in your life, it will infuse you with delight no matter what the situation.

How to discover purpose

As a pastor, I find it challenging to come up with new material every week for essentially the same crowd. During the years when I worked with John MacArthur (pastor/teacher of Grace Community Church in Sun Valley, California) I was amazed at how he did this so effectively, accurately, thoroughly, and passionately every Sunday—morning and evening. One day we stood outside the Denver airport waiting to be picked up by our hosts. He told me that preaching was to him, "a blessed bondage." Blessed because he had the privilege of being paid to study God's Word. Bondage because, ready or not, Sunday always comes.

And, yes, Sunday always comes. It's as if a gun goes off every Monday morning. A downhill race begins. I am running, with a big boulder chasing me down the slope. The boulder is the finished sermon. The goal is to get to Sunday before Sunday gets to me.

It is hard work to study the text thoroughly and exegete it accurately every week. Of course, my printed outline has to be put together and in the bulletins ahead of time. Usually illustrations and an occasional humorous anecdote complement my weekly "work of art." Eventually, the content is essentially done. Then, I take one final step. I print the rough draft and look at all the things I am telling our people they ought to do. Next to each of these I write the three letters, "YBH." This stands for "Yes—but how?"

Ultimately it is the work of the Holy Spirit to apply truth to the hearts of the recipients. I also know that I must ask Him to apply the sermon to my own heart as well, before I get up to obligate others to obey. Frankly, this is one of the most grueling exercises I engage in every week.

In asking, *Why am I here?* we have looked at the differences between purpose and mission. We've examined biblical examples of purpose. The benefits of purpose have encouraged our hearts. Now, it's time to ask, "Yes, but how?"

Commit!

First, commit to an authentic relationship with God through Christ. It's not enough to know about God or to come to church. Information or sermons cannot give you purpose. Only God through Jesus Christ can do that. It's what the Gospel, the Good News, is proclaiming. The good news is that Jesus Christ came to give you purpose and to forgive you for sin: past, present, and future. He enables you to exchange all that you are for all that He is and to have the very Spirit of God through Christ living in your life. In John 10:10 we see that He came that we "might have life, and might have it abundantly."

Consider!

In the process of discovering purpose, consider what really matters in the final analysis. What do you think of when the name of Richard Nixon is mentioned? Billy Graham? O. J. Simpson? Mother Teresa? Princess Diana? Madonna? Saddam Hussein? Do all these names evoke the same response? Certainly not. But their legacy in life is obvious, for better or for worse.

Yet it's wise to remember that life on earth is not the final scoreboard. The scoreboard that matters is in heaven, and this is what you need to live for. Think beyond this life and focus on the final analysis of eternity. This is what will ultimately matter.

It's really a matter of arithmetic. Figure a normal life span on earth is around eighty years. Eternity is more than eighty, more than eight hundred, more than eight thousand, eight million, eight trillion. It's forever; so why in the world would anyone live earth's brief span of time with any purpose that didn't primarily connect with eternity? Yet we do it all the time.

We can live our lives for things that really have no significance on the final scoreboard of existence. Second Corinthians 5:10 reminds us that "we must all appear before the judgment seat of Christ, that each one may be recompensed for his deeds in the body, according to what he has done, whether good or bad."

We should evaluate life, as did King Solomon in the book of Ecclesiastes. This man was richer than Howard Hughes, Bill Gates, and Sam Walton all put together. He was one of the richest men of all time, with all pleasures at his disposal, yet he set out to find the value and purpose of life.

He searched through physical gratification, possessions, education, and success. What was his conclusion? Vanity, vanity, all was vanity. Remember what he said at the end of this book? When it's all been said and done, "fear God and keep His commandments, because this applies to every person. For God will bring every act to judgment, everything which is hidden, whether it is good or evil."

Solomon had tried it all, searched it thoroughly. His advice? Play for eternity, run for the prize that matters. Don't be detoured by the temporary, because eternity is a mighty long time.

Construct!

When discovering your purpose, construct your conclusion on the foundation of your theology and identity. Here we are again, full circle to who God is and who you are. In the passage of 2 Corinthians 5:11–21, Paul reveals his foundation. He says that he knows the fear of the Lord and the love of Christ. He recognizes that he is now a new creature in Christ and has been given the identity of being an ambassador for Christ. True purpose is not what Mom or Dad thinks, nor what your boss or you think. Worthwhile purpose begins and ends with who God is and who you are in Christ.

Concretize!

After committing to a relationship with God through Christ, considering what really matters in the final analysis, and constructing your purpose on a foundation of truth, you need to concretize. This is one of my favorite words. It means to make it clear, absolute, concrete-solid. In other words, write it down. Whenever the Lord wanted to communicate something to be remembered, the directions were to preserve the words. To Moses, the instruction was, "Write it down." Solomon told his son to bind the wise sayings on his fingers and to write them on his heart. We should do the same.

It's insightful to make clear to yourself and others why you are here. When you write and think clearly and specifically, you gain a guide that works like a gyroscope. When circumstances knock you off balance, there is a readable reminder that helps you stabilize again.

Clarify!

Another essential part of the discovery process is to clarify your purposes through review and revision on a regular basis. I emphasize the revision part, as I have revised my purposes several times. It's because of this verse, "It is God who is at work in you, both to will and to work for His good pleasure" (Philippians 2:13). Notice that it says that God *is* at work, not *was*. So it's not a product, set in unyielding stone. It is still a process. Writing your personal purpose statements gives them more substance. Revision reflects the growth in your understanding of God, yourself, and the exact purposes He has for you in the various dimensions of your life.

I like to do this at the beginning of each year, taking a morning or an afternoon, just to focus on how God may have given me more clarity on my roles and purposes, as a new slice of life begins. Occasionally, I will take a personal retreat and make any necessary revisions once I have unplugged from the busyness of life and slowed down enough to think deeply. However you choose to do it—just do it. It will be worth your time and attention.

Consider!

When God tells His people in the Scriptures to "consider your ways" (Haggai 1:5, 7), He's not just suggesting an occasional moment of warm reflection. He is not intimating that, when we have nothing better to do, we might want to give some casual thought to His ideas. No, His intent is that we engage ourselves fully in an all-out evaluation, based on His commands and plans for our lives. Just as the Jews in Haggai's day had lost focus, failing to live out their identity and God-given purposes, so can we.

As noted in the introduction of this book, our greatest battles are fought daily on the private battleground of our inner man. We must consider every day the purposes of God for our lives. "Why am I here?" is indeed one of the absolutely essential questions for strategic daily renewal.

As I have done, I challenge you to keep your written purposes in the flyleaf of your Bible—or in the opening pages of your daily planner. This kind of daily mental focus keeps your life focused. Write them on index cards and carry them in your pocket or purse. Paste them on your bathroom mirror. Memorize these purposes. Call them to mind throughout the day.

I've heard various speakers talk about the difference between diffused light and focused light. Diffused light is weak and limited—like a 60-watt lightbulb in your lamp. Focused light is powerful—like a laser beam. Thinking about purpose is good. Beginning the process of integrating your answers with the foundational essentials of theology and identity is vital. Writing out your purposes is even better. Reflecting on these things will keep them current. But, until your personal answers to the question, "Why am I here?" become a daily habit, you may very well have the impact of a faint 60-watt bulb in the corner of a room. Better to be a laser beam, cutting through the darkness of life—radiant, powerful, and living to the glory of God.

A personal guide to defining your purposes in life

Your eternal purpose

The Westminster Catechism says that "the chief end of man is to glorify God and to enjoy Him forever." Write a statement that you can make your own in the space below:

Your earthly purpose

Study the following passages, which describe Christ's earthly purpose (or mission). Matthew 5:17, 20:28; Mark 10:45; Luke 4:43, 12:49, 19:10; John 6:33, 9:39, 10:10, 12:47, 17:4, 18:37, and 1 Timothy 1:15. What strikes you as being especially meaningful to your life? Write it below.

If you could write a summary of your life that would some-day be chiseled on your tombstone, what would it say?

When you arrive in heaven, what would you most like the Lord to say about your life?

Using the material in the previous three questions, write a mis-sion statement describing your earthly purpose for being here.

Your explicit Purposes

Review the discussion on the explicit purposes of your life on pages 102–103.

Using the following chart, list the key roles you fulfill in life. In the adjoining space, begin to craft a purpose statement for each function. Note the example.

Role	Purpose
Father	To teach my children to love God by modeling and instructing them in godliness, and to demonstrate relational love by loving their mother sacrificially every day.

Question 4

"What really matters?"

Ideas go booming through the world louder than cannons. Thoughts are mightier than armies. Principles have achieved more victories than horsemen or chariots.
W. M. Paxton[1]

Back of every noble life there are principles that have fashioned it.
George H. Lorimer[2]

If anyone competes as an athlete, he does not win the prize unless he competes according to the rules.
2 Timothy 2:5

A special edition of *USA Today* featured "The Debate: Values in School." It included this quote from former President Reagan: "We don't expect children to discover principles of calculus on their own, but some would give them no guidance when it comes to ethics, morality, and values."[3] Similarly, columnist William Raspberry wrote, "In our zeal to get religion out of the classroom, we threw out morality as well."

On the other side of the issue, an assistant school superintendent from Connecticut said, "It is outside the scope of our charge to teach morals. Whose version of ethics would we use?" A home economics textbook entitled *Today's Teen* states a similar viewpoint: "Too strict a conscience may make you feel different and unpopular. None of these feelings belong to a healthy personality."

A high school class was asked if it is right or wrong to return a lost purse containing $1,000 to the rightful owner. The majority of the students thought it would be foolish.

In the same issue of *USA Today* mentioned above, a cartoon of young George Washington was printed that illustrates the plight of many students today. He had just cut down the cherry tree and was saying to his father, "Dad, my teacher says I cannot tell a lie, I cannot tell the truth, and I cannot tell the difference."

We all may remember the much-publicized story involving President Bill Clinton and a White House intern, Monica Lewinsky. Charges were made that the President had asked Lewinsky to lie under oath. In a poll conducted by the Gallup organization at the time, Americans were asked if Clinton ought to resign if he did, in fact, subvert the legal process in this way. It was shocking to learn that virtually half of those questioned said "no."[4] The basic theory of this segment of our culture is that, as long as the man in charge keeps the economy strong and keeps my life comfortable, who cares if he breaks the law? As long as he does his job we don't seem to care whether or not our national leader lives by a set of solid moral values!

Today, we live in an age of moral relativism. It's found in business, education, and politics. We also experience it in family life and even in religious circles. In American society, when it comes to values and issues of principle, our feet are floating in midair.

George Barna, when conducting one of his national polls, found that 71 percent of the responders do not believe in absolute truth. With feedback like that, what kind of life philosophy are people choosing? Whose values are we embracing?

In an insightful book by Hunter Lewis, entitled *A Question of Values*, he notes that we concoct or derive our value system from six basic areas. The first is *authority*, or that which is passed down to us as authoritative and true. Next is our own *logic*, then our own *experience*, *emotion*, and *intuition*. Finally comes *science*, which tries to unravel both the invisible and the visible.[5]

Reason would seem to indicate that when we remove authority, or that which is absolutely true, we are left with a limited and subjective value system. The only tools left for constructing a value system are personal experience, emotion, intuition, and the fact-producing investigations of science. Small wonder that our top leaders live under the dark cloud of scandalous living, that our families are falling apart at the seams, that our churches are weak, and that our hearts sometimes feel hopeless.

Your philosophy of life—a set of working values

Some of us may have taken a philosophy class in college, and when we finished it we were more confused than when we started. Heads nod, eyes roll, and one wonders, *Just what is philosophy, anyhow, and what difference will it make in my life?*

The word comes from two Greek terms, *philos* which means "love" and *sophia* which means "wisdom." So *philosophy* is the "love of wisdom." The Bible often speaks of God's truth and connects it with the need for acquiring and keeping sound wisdom (Proverbs 1–9). It is the love of God's truth that results in wise practical living. That is what true wisdom is.

A philosophy of life is a set of personal convictions that cannot be compromised.

Let's use this working definition for philosophy: A love for wisdom that results in a system of principles, based on truth, which form a foundation and a framework for living. Your philosophy, in essence, is a set of personal convictions that cannot be compromised. It can also be described as a value system.

When we think of someone who is a principled person, what characteristics come to mind? A person who knows what he or she believes and who lives it might come to mind. Such people have a well-thought-out set of uncompromising principles upon which they base their lives. It's a value system for making decisions.

What if someone were to come up and ask, "Can you give me your philosophy of life in two minutes or less?" Could you identify some nonnegotiable principles that are real for you and that have been woven into the fabric of your daily existence? Are they so clear and dominant in your thinking that they are part of the foundation and framework of your daily life? Do you have a definite awareness that your principles are derived from the Word of God? Maybe not yet since many people falter when it comes to thinking about and living out their most closely held principles of life.

Perhaps a sports analogy might better explain the problem. I know that I am a Christian, so I'm playing on a team called the *Saints*. I know who I am—a wide receiver. I know what my mission is: to win the game. But if I don't know the rules, and if I don't play or live by those rules, I am not going to be very effective.

Paul reminds us about how we play the game: "If anyone competes as an athlete, he does not win the prize unless he competes according to the rules" (2 Timothy 2:5).

What rules? The athlete's own rules? Society's? Rules based on worldly theories? No. God's rules. Do we know the rules, live by them, and are we able to articulate them? If not, now is the time to develop a guiding philosophy of life.

Declared versus demonstrated

People exhibit their own philosophy of life from two aspects. One is what I call a *declared philosophy*. If an individual were to articulate it, he or she would say, "Well, it is this and it is that." A more specific example would be, "Well, it is God first, family second, and me third." This is often heard in Christian gatherings. We call it J.O.Y.—Jesus, others, yourself. When we say this, we are declaring the principles we embrace. This is easy to say but more difficult to model.

The other aspect is what I call a *demonstrated philosophy*. While our declared philosophy is what we say, our demonstrated philosophy shows what really matters to us by the way we actually live.

It doesn't take a rocket scientist to figure out that some of us are philosophical schizophrenics; we often say one thing and do another. We exhibit a split sense of understanding and reality every time we verbalize one thing but live another.

It reminds me of a story about a young, highly-principled, unmarried seminarian. He just graduated from seminary, and he knew what he believed. He valued sincerity, truth, and honesty. That was, until one day when he boarded a plane. Sitting there, he noticed a beautiful young woman coming down the aisle. He found it hard not to stare. Sure enough, she sat right down beside him. She then opened her Bible and started to read. "There is a God in heaven," he said to himself, "and He is smiling upon me!"

He started a conversation with her, having first checked to make sure she had no wedding ring. After a little casual conversation, he decided to be more direct and asked, "What kind of men do you like?"

"That's an interesting question," she replied. "This may be unexpected, but I like Native American men. They really have a sense of heritage and history. They know who they are and they're powerful.

"But," she continued, "I've known some Jewish fellows also, and what a sense of morality and heritage and principle they have. I really enjoy their friendship. Still, to be very honest with you, my favorite kind of guy is just a country boy. They're so honest and down-to-earth and easy to get to know."

The seminarian was deep in thought when she decided to ask him a question. "By the way, what is your name?" she said. The principled young man moved closer to her and replied, "Oh, my name is Geronimo Steinbeck, but my friends just call me 'Bubba.' "

We could call this situation ethics. Most of us, if we thought about it, live somewhere between our declared and demonstrated philosophy of life. Just like some of the people of Jesus' time. He spoke to them about the very same inconsistency when He said, "Not everyone who *says* to Me, 'Lord, Lord,' will enter the kingdom of heaven; but he who *does* the will of My Father, who is in heaven"(Matthew 7:21, emphasis added).

Paul's letter to Titus speaks of those who profess one thing but do another: "They profess to know God, but by their deeds they deny Him . . ." (Titus 1:16). Jesus also said, "Why do you call Me, 'Lord, Lord,' and do not do what I say?" (Luke 6:46).

The task for us, if we are going to live an integrated, meaningful life, is to have a system of principles in which our declared and the demonstrated philosophies are consistent as a whole instead of being two contradictory statements. Such is the life of integrity.

This idea can be represented in the form of an equation:

Declared + Demonstrated = Integrity
Declared − Demonstrated = Hypocrisy

When my demonstrated philosophy and declared philosophy fit together in harmony, the result is a life of integrity. When they differ, it produces hypocrisy.

Saying one thing and doing another is a form of deception that increases with every episode. Deception is a downhill road that inevitably dead-ends into an undesirable destination. It is not enough to have a great statement about who God is and a firm understanding of who we are in Him and why we're here. We must have a biblical philosophy of life that is integrated with the rest of our foundation.

Former Senior Editor of *Christianity Today*, V. Gilbert Beers, said, "A person of integrity is one who has an established system of principles against which all of his life is judged."[6] Perhaps some real-life examples of life philosophies in action will be of help.

New Testament clips of values in action

Let's begin with a positive illustration from the Gospels. Here we find Jesus, at the beginning His ministry, clearly demonstrating His philosophy of life. In those pre-dawn moments, Satan came and said, "If You are the Son of God, command that these stones become bread" (Matthew 4:3). Being tempted in the area of physical appetite after forty days without food, Jesus could have replied, "Yes, I am hungry. I think that's a good idea." Instead, He counteracted the temptation and demonstrated His philosophy by answering, "It is written, 'Man shall not live on bread alone, but on every word that proceeds out of the mouth of God' " (Matthew 4:4). Quoting from the Law (Deuteronomy 8:3), He declared and demonstrated an integrated value system.

If situation ethics had been His value system, He would have changed those stones into bread and satisfied His hunger. Instead, He stated the truth that real satisfaction comes from obedience, not self-gratification.

Satan then tried to tempt Him with personal gain by going to a high place and saying, "Throw Yourself down; for it is written, 'He will give His angels charge concerning You'; and 'on their hands they will bear You up . . .' " (Matthew 4:6). Cunningly using the verse out of context, Satan offered Jesus an opportunity that would have been quite spectacular. Still He responded, "On the other hand, it is written, 'You shall not tempt the Lord your God' " (Matthew 4:7). In effect, Jesus again answered "no" with the knowledge that true gain comes only from doing the will of God.

One more time, when offered the power and glory of all the kingdoms of the world, He was tempted. Declining again, Jesus said, "Begone, Satan! For it is written, 'You shall worship the Lord your God, and serve Him only.' " (Matthew 4:10). He manifested the principle that real power is in worshiping God alone. Anything less is mere emptiness.

Jesus demonstrated a clear philosophy of life that was immediately apparent in the crisis moments of His life. Sometime afterward, He taught His disciples these very same values while on a mountain (Matthew 5–7).

In the Sermon on the Mount Jesus taught that real happiness is not found in what is seen, but in that which is unseen. Real happiness is not what happens to you, but in you. Real impact comes from living for God, not for yourself. Real integrity is an issue of the heart, not of words. What Jesus said was validated by His life. That's integrity.

For a negative illustration, we have the Pharisees. Jesus had just pronounced seven woes upon these religious leaders. He revealed the great disparity in their lives; that they lived their declared philosophy of life only when it was advantageous, to achieve selfish ends. He said to them, "Even so you too outwardly appear righteous to men, but inwardly you are full of hypocrisy and lawlessness" (Matthew 23:28).

In the Bible, we have these two radical illustrations, one very positive, one very negative. We all live somewhere between, hopefully attempting to become more consistent in declaring as well as demonstrating our philosophy of life.

A personal illustration of practical family values

I am on a journey as well. I have developed my personal values, using the acrostic from my first name. It is in the front of my planning notebook. I think about it regularly and am still adding Scripture verses and detailed applications to each principle. Over the last six years, with regard to family, I have put together a declared set of values or principles. After each principle is a little slogan. I've actually used these slogans to teach the principles to my children. They have memorized them. I have also given each of them a professionally-printed, three-ring binder that contains the full text of the verses. These have become real treasures to them.

We talk about these values often in the course of daily life. Perhaps they could be called a "family philosophy."

Principle One *(Spirituality)*
    Love God with all your heart
    (Matthew 22:37–38)

Principle Two *(Service)*
    Love and serve other people
    (Matthew 22:39–40; Galatians 5:13–14)

Principle Three *(Renewal)*
Pray and read your Bible every day
(Matthew 4:4; 1 Thessalonians 5:17)

Principle Four *(Obedience)*
Please and obey God—no matter what
(1 Samuel 15:22; 2 Corinthians 5:9)

Principle Five *(Honesty)*
Always tell the truth
(Psalm 15:2; Ephesians 4:15, 25)

Principle Six *(Credibility)*
Always keep your word
(Psalm 15:4)

Principle Seven *(Endurance)*
Finish what you start
(2 Timothy 4:7; Hebrews 12:1–2)

Principle Eight *(Self-management)*
Use your time wisely
(Psalm 39:4; Ephesians 5:15–16)

Principle Nine *(Excellence)*
Always look your best
(1 Corinthians 6:19–20)

Principle Ten *(Dependence)*
Pray for wisdom every day
(1 Kings 3:9–10; Proverbs 2:1–8; James 1:5

Principle Eleven *(Purity)*
Always have a pure mind, a grateful heart, and a clear
conscience
(Philippians 4:8; 1 Thessalonians 5:18; 2 Timothy 1:3)

Principle Twelve *(Enthusiasm)*
Give it all you've got!
(Ecclesiastes 9:10; 1 Corinthians 15:58; Colossians 3:23–24)

As you can see, some of these principles set high standards. Like number nine: Always look your best. Isn't that pious? But these are things that matter to our family. Love God first, love others; and if you love others, you'll serve them. We hope our children will remember the twelve principles that matter in our home.

What about the demonstrational aspect of our family philosophy? If you know my children, they have made some progress, and have the opportunity to make more. So do I, but it is our desire to always be directed by this guiding system of principles.

Not having a well-defined family philosophy reminds me of the story of a family who sought to come up with a name for their new ranch. They had just sold their home in the city, had decided to raise cattle, and were debating about what to name their ranch.

After they were settled in their new location, and had bought a large herd, a friend came to visit. Out of curiosity, he asked, "What did you finally name this ranch?" The father hesitated, then said, "Well, I wanted to name it 'The Flying W,' but my wife liked 'The Suzy Q.' Our sons suggested 'The Bar J,' and our daughter preferred 'The Lazy Y.' So, we call it, 'The Flying W, Suzy Q, Bar J, Lazy Y Ranch.'" The visitor looked around, then asked, "So, where are the cattle?" The father again hesitated, then replied, "None of them survived the branding."[7]

Are values guiding your church?

Sometimes the local church is like that. It can become a mosaic of opinion, and many churches don't survive the brandings of personal opinion, ideas, whims, and wants. Even a church needs to develop a philosophy that says, "This is what we believe, and this is why." Not just in terms of theology, but also in terms of practice.

When choosing a church, be sure to get clear answers to the essential questions. One is, "What do you believe about the Bible?" Is it just a nice little story of collected myths, or is it the inspired, authoritative Word of God? You may want to know what they believe about worship and leadership. Do they follow the nice-guy syndrome, where anybody who is willing is put into leadership? Or do they insist that a leader be a godly, exemplary person who knows the Word of God and is committed to teaching, equipping, and discipling?

Other important questions are their beliefs about the congregation and evangelism. Do they allow a philosophy of "pew-potatoism," or do they believe that every member is to participate in the work of the ministry (Ephesians 4:11–13)? Do they think the preacher's up there with a big fishing pole, or do they equip each person to take a fishing pole and cast the baited hook where the fish are? All these questions can be answered when a church has declared its values clearly and concisely. Hopefully, they are also being demonstrated with integrity.

During the Gulf War in 1991, most everyone was amazed and impressed by news network video footage of Allied missiles hitting strategic sites in the country of Iraq. These high-powered weapons were guided by a sophisticated system of computerized intelligence. From great distances these high-tech sticks of dynamite hit their targets with extraordinary precision.

On the other hand, we recall Saddam Hussein's hit-and-miss scud missiles. In a recent tour to the Holy Land, we drove through the area of Tel Aviv where many of those missiles landed. I called it "scud row." Our Israeli tour guide pointed out that these missiles landed many miles from their intended target. They lacked a proper guidance system and turned out to be a danger to civilians rather than a strategic military strike.

Whether in your own life, family, church, or work—it is vital to ask the question, "What Really Matters?" Without focused consideration about and careful implementation of your values, life may fly about like an unpredictable scud missile and wander off course. As a result, many of your efforts may not count in the battle that matters the most—the battle of personal integrity.

Developing a philosophy of life

I grew up loving and playing football. Starting in fourth grade I began suiting up in shoulder pads, helmet, mouthpiece, cleats, and the rest of the uniform. This passion continued through high school. It would have paid my way through college had it not been for some serious injuries during my senior year. When the doctor informed me that to accept the scholarship and continue playing would involve two shoulder surgeries, I promptly hung up the pads and retired at the ripe old age of eighteen.

Because I played football, I understand the game. I know the rules and recognize the signals of the referees. But when it comes to sporting events like soccer, hockey, or the various competitions of the "X-games," count me out. I don't understand what's going on.

In some ways, people are like the various sports. The exact applications and strategies are different, just as people differ from one another, but the fundamental core values are the same. Regardless of the sport, the essential values behind the penalties and guidelines involve fairness, maximum competition, ethical sportsmanship, scorekeeping, basic safety, and (of course) winning or losing.

For all of us, the essential ground rules are the same. The way we play the game and apply those fundamentals in the practical arena of life may look different. But we still must take the time to decide where the boundaries are, what fairness means, what constitutes a penalty, and what it means to score. So, how do you define your rules for the contest of life?

The three "R's"—reflect, read, and (w)rite

First, reflect on what is important, what really matters to you. As you do this, read the Bible. The process of reflecting and reading will help you articulate your declared philosophy of life. Then start to write it down. Clarify and make specific the principles of your life that you will not compromise. In the future, you likely will revise them, but here is the place to begin.

You could choose one of many ways to formulate a value system or philosophy of life. The foundation is truth—the Word of God. Of the many verses in the sixty-six books of Scripture, you may want to choose themes and key passages that have most influenced you in your personal reading and study. Take paper and pen and start brainstorming on the theme of practical principles for living. Be patient and open to the Lord as you do so; it may take many months to formulate your ideas in a careful and applicable way.

This is an exercise to be done in the same spirit as that mentioned when, in Deuteronomy 11:18–21, God told the leaders and fathers of Israel through Moses:

> "You shall therefore impress these words of mine on your heart and on your soul; and you shall bind them as a sign on your hand, and they shall be as frontals on your forehead. And you shall teach them to your sons, talking of them when you sit in your house and when you walk along the road and when you lie down and when you rise up. And you shall write them on the doorposts of your house and on your gates, so that your days and the days of your sons may be multiplied on the land which the Lord swore to your fathers to give them, as long as the heavens remain above the earth."

The intention of this exercise is to remember, practice, and reproduce these values. Keep that in mind as you journey through the process.

Build on your foundation

Now is the time to review your theology, identity, and purposes in life. Think about the principles that you have been formulating and choose the ones that are most consistent with this foundation. Write down any new thoughts that come from this process.

What have you admired in others?

Next, who are your mentors, models, or heroes? Some may be biblical, some historic, while others may be personal acquaintances or family members. I have a "wall of fame" in my office: ten pictures that include family members and Christian leaders I know. Under each picture I've noted each person's outstanding qualities. I review them regularly and also pray for each of these "modern-day heroes." It has been said that we should cultivate in ourselves the qualities we most admire in others. This is a part of your formulation process.

Seek honest feedback

Now ask some friends who know you well and can be "truth tellers" of what they see as the deeply held qualities and commitments in your life. Add these to your list. Remember, this is a brainstorming process. Let the list grow without much critical evaluation. Eventually you'll do some synthesizing and combining of qualities that overlap each other.

Refining your list

At some point the list will become quite extensive. After prayerful prioritization, choose anywhere from six to a dozen of the most important qualities of character. A one-word description or brief phrase that captures the essence of each quality is your goal. Then, write a couple clarifying sentences after each one. For future review, keep it clear, condensed, memorable, and meaningful.

Organize to memorize

Having thought deeply about your guiding principles, it may be worthwhile to organize them in an easy-to-remember form. For example, someone might organize a philosophy of life around the acrostic, C-H-A-R-A-C-T-E-R. It might look like this:

C—Consistency
H—Honesty
A—Authentic spirituality
R—Relationships (family/friends)
A—Attitude
C—Compassion
T—Truth-telling
E—Enthusiasm
R—Resilience

Of course, these words are general. A full philosophy will contain some practical description for each one and Scripture references that support them.

In Paul's second letter to Timothy he said, "Continue in the things you have learned and become convinced of . . ." (2 Timothy 3:14). He was instructing this young man in an age when deceivers, evil men, and impostors were going from bad to worse. It was a society like our own, full of people whose feet are floating in midair. In stark contrast to this worldview, Paul reminded Timothy to come back to basic principles. These principles are comprised of the wisdom that leads to salvation through Jesus Christ.

Paul reminded him that "All Scripture is inspired by God and profitable for teaching, for reproof, for correction, for training in righteousness . . ." (2 Timothy 3:16). God's Word would equip him to stand strong. Paul instructed Timothy not to compromise the truth, because the day was coming when people would have itching ears and they would seek teachers who would say whatever they want to hear. They also would turn aside to myths, to a philosophy without any mooring. This is why, even today, you need to articulate carefully what you believe, and then keep holding on to it.

Learning to live by the values you value

Someone has said that an *expert* is anyone, with anything to say, who is at least fifty miles from home. In other words, if you get far enough from the context in which you live your daily life, and among some folks with whom there is no real accountability, you can act like a know-it-all—and get away with it. The warning here is that we may impress people who don't know us, but lack integrity with those who do. This reminds us that our reputation is what people think we are; character is what God knows us to be. Living without integrity is like a wandering scud missile, or like a cheap bottle rocket. We won't hit the mark.

The objective is not to be an "expert" when it comes to values. Our aim is to be an example. To that end we must practice a regimen of brutal honesty and ongoing evaluation. The issue here is: "How do I *live* this system of values?"

It's possible to be deceived. James hits us with a double-barreled exhortation when he reminds us: "Prove yourselves doers of the word, and not merely hearers who delude themselves. . . . If anyone thinks himself to be religious, and yet does not bridle his tongue but deceives his own heart, this man's religion is worthless" (James 1: 22, 26). We must constantly make sure that our actions, attitudes, and words are moving in the direction of what we have understood to be right and true.

Again keep in mind that this is a regular, preferably a daily, process. The vulnerability of the heart to conform to the world's system of values is very subtle. In the midst of thousands of daily distractions our minds can easily drift out of focus regarding the principles that matter the most to us. We must constantly evaluate: Am I merely declaring these principles, or does my life also demonstrate them?

Paul understood this as he prayed that the believers in Colossae would embrace God's wisdom, God's principles, and live them out into fruitfulness (Colossians 1:9–10). To do this requires that we look at the way we are living (Colossians 1:23, 28). Are we playing by God's rules or are we being held captive by philosophies that aren't biblical (Colossians 2:4–10)?

Test One: my thoughts

To test your values, a good question to ask is, "What dominates my thinking?" As a man thinks in his heart, so he is (Proverbs 23:7). Whatever is dominating your thoughts is what really matters to you. You need to decide if these thoughts are based on God's revealed truths. If not, then it's wise to say, "This is not right. These dominating thoughts are not true, not biblical. These are not the values to which I want to commit my life."

Test Two: my time

Another question is, "Where do I spend my time?" I know people who say in their declared philosophy, "Family is a priority." Still, they're never home. And when they are home, they are not "home." In actuality, family is not a priority for them. They need to look at their time allotment and at what they're doing. This is true for all of us in many areas. We need to think about how and where we are spending our time.

Test Three: my money

Then there's the question of how we spend money. I believe you can tell what matters to someone by simply looking at his or her calendar and checkbook. Jesus said, "Where your treasure is, there will your heart be also" (Matthew 6:21). Many say, "I love God's kingdom, so I give one percent of my income." Here is a disparity, because if you love something you will give it priority. You can't love without giving, without sacrifice, and if He's not first in the financial area of your life, then what you demonstrate contradicts your declared philosophy.

You can tell more about a person's Christianity by his reactions than by his actions.

Test Four: my reactions

Here is another question that might help: "How do I react to the unexpected?" Usually a person can calculate behavior in advance, but when something unexpected happens, one reacts in accordance to what he or she really believes and what really matters. During my high school days, I remember being quite intrigued with the writings of Watchman Nee. In a series of practical lectures, he dedicated an entire chapter to the issue of "The Christian Reaction." He essentially stated that you can tell much more about a person's Christianity by their reactions, than by their actions.[8]

Although we say we want to be servants, we may revert to pride, self-protection, or even winning at any cost. Gordon MacDonald said it this way: "You can tell whether you're becoming a servant by how you act when people treat you like one."[9] How do I react to the unexpected? This will demonstrate what my real philosophy is.

Test Five: my friends

I've heard it said that pride is like bad breath; everyone knows you have it except you! Not only is this true of pride, but of many other qualities in our lives that become blind spots. If you are really serious about getting a read on how you demonstrate your declared philosophy, ask yourself, "What would those who know me best, and love me most, say is true about me if they knew I could handle it?" Those closest to us hear our words, but they also see our lives. They are often more aware of the reality that sometimes our actions and our words do not correspond. I love John Maxwell's definition of *success:* "success is when those who know me the best, respect me the most."

Coming to terms with the gap

There is a story about two older women who were in an English cemetery that was rather crowded with gravesites. They came upon one headstone that read, "Here lies John Smith, a politician and an honest man." One of the women said to the other, "Good heavens! Isn't it awful that they had to bury two people in the same grave!"

My purpose in telling this story is not to pick on politicians, because some are honest. But the possibility exists that in some dimension of life, we could be buried with a similar headstone reading, "Here lies [so and so], a husband and an honest man," and someone who knew him would say, "Oh, two people in one grave." We need to examine our lives for any disparity that may be present now so that passersby won't stumble over the message on our headstone.

When I was growing up, one principle of life in our home was "self-honesty" or "no-excuse living." My parents would often say, "Daniel, you do what you want to do." This would effectively defuse my lame explanations for not doing my chores or homework. Basically, it was a call to look at my heart and see the disparity between my words and my deeds.

This is an essential part of living out a consistent set of values. It does no good to have an elaborate declaration of values when we have a poor demonstration of them. When what we do contradicts what we say, it's time for a reality check. Either I need to cast myself fresh upon God's grace with a heart of honest repentance or make necessary adjustments in my declared philosophy statement.

Closing the gap by His grace

When you've considered all of these tests and used them as a guide for examining the gap, it's time to subordinate what you do to what you say, in order to bring the authority of truth into your life. Invite the Lord to close the gap. In a disciplined way, constantly subject your mind for renewal in the knowledge of the truth and things that He has already declared important. Commit yourself to those things. Paul exhorted believers with these directives: "Be renewed in the spirit of your mind" (Ephesians 4:23). To the Colossians he said, "Put on the new self who is being renewed to a true knowledge according to the image of the One who created him" (Colossians 3:10).

The value of living with integrity in values

Tony Campolo once described the results from an insightful social research poll conducted on fifty people, all over the age of ninety-five. They were asked, "What would you do differently if you had life to live over again?" The top three answers were these: I would reflect more, risk more, and do more things that would live on after I'm dead.[10]

A Christian application of these responses might be, "I would take more time to clarify the principles that really matter. Then, after examining their eternal value, I would take the risk and boldly live out my life based on these principles." This is the collective voice of fifty people with ninety-five years of experience. A person doesn't have to live that long to learn these lessons. It's never too late to stop and clarify what matters, to base them solidly upon the truth of God, and then to act upon them with integrity.

Those who live meaningful lives are people of deep conviction. To develop conviction you must slow down and ask yourself what matters. Then, check to see if there is a disparity between what you say and what you do. In the beginning, it may have to be a daily process. With consistent practice, though, the principles will become clear both in your words and life.

Bertrand Russell, the Nobel Prize-winning philosopher and mathematician from England, is a familiar figure to all who have lived during the first half of this century. In 1890, at age eighteen, he declared himself an atheist. From then on his "theology," identity, mission, and philosophy made him a topic of controversy around the world. His disdain of God, hatred for Christianity, opposition to war, and inordinate advocacy of loose morality shaped his entire life experience.

While living by these values, he was married four times and had many lovers. Dora, his second wife, was pregnant at the time of their marriage with the first of two children they would conceive. Consistent with his philosophy of life, Russell believed in open marriage. However, after Dora bore two children by another man, Russell could not stand the "torture" of family life and they divorced.

By his fourth marriage, Russell again reaped the generational fruit of his flawed value system. Russell's son, John, and his wife, decided they were also tired of family life and they separated. They also abandoned their three daughters and Russell had the responsibility of raising these grandchildren in his later years. John eventually suffered a breakdown.

The bright spot in all of this is that Russell's daughter, Kate, married an American who became an Episcopal minister. In a dramatic departure from the life-views of her father, Kate and her husband went to Uganda as missionaries.

In his delightful book, *What Happened to Their Kids*, Malcolm Forbes quotes Kate as crediting her father for her religious conversion. She speaks of the impossible demands imposed by her father and how, as children, they were "loaded down with inescapable and, to us, inexplicable guilt." As a result, she chose a better theology, identity, purpose, and philosophy.

She did not see her father (one of the most famous atheists of his time) as being entirely irreligious. In looking back on his life, she noted in her memoirs, "I believe myself that his whole life was a search for God. Or for those who prefer less personal terms, for absolute certainty."[11]

This sad account reminds us of the lifelong result of fundamental choices. As you choose your "rules to live by" remember the impact your choices will have on your life, and on those around you—for better or for worse.

A personal guide to developing your values

Formulating your DECLARED values:

Reflect:
In the space below, begin to write brief descriptions of the convictions you feel are most important in your life. These are principles that you hope you would never compromise in the course of daily living. This is a brainstorming type of exercise so be open and creative as you write.

Research the Word:

Over a period of weeks, perhaps months, begin to keep track of the passages of Scripture that have most influenced your life. These may be favorite verses from childhood. Perhaps they will be verses that have been vital in past decisions. Maybe they will be fairly recent discoveries from your reading. Write the references in the space below along with a brief description of the values taught in each passage.

Review your foundation:

Go back and review your theology, identity, and purpose statements. Consider the kind of guiding principles you would need to keep before you to live out these ideals. Do this exercise many times, over a span of weeks. Each time, write down any new values that come to mind.

Revisit your "Most Admired List"

In the space below, write the names of the people who have most influenced your life. These people may be parents, spiritual leaders, friends, or associates. They may be heroes from many years ago whose biographies have touched you deeply. Next to each name, write the character qualities that stand out to you.

Don't forget to consider the life and character of the Lord
Jesus Christ. He is the ultimate model.

Receive honest feedback:
Tell some trusted relatives or friends what you are working
on. Ask them to be practical and honest with you. What would
they say are your guiding principles in life, based on the way
you have lived before them? In the space below, write the
answers you receive.

Ready to synthesize:
Now review the lists you have made in the previous exercises. Look for recurring themes. Notice values that are similar
and can be combined. Try to summarize the results. Hopefully
you can end up with a list of five, ten, or fifteen core values that
you can begin to clarify for your own list.

"Organize to memorize"
This final step may take some time. You may want to organize
your selected values into a form that will be easy to remember
and readily apply to your life. It may be an acrostic, where the
first letter of the words are arranged to spell something meaning-

ful to you. It may be in alphabetical order. You may choose an alliteration, where all the words begin with the same letter. It is up to you. Use the space below to work on your final format.

(This same process can be used to formulate guiding principles in other areas of your life [family, work, church].)

Investigating your DEMONSTRATED values:
Along the way you will want to take time for a "reality check." Our ideals guide us toward a higher level of living. However, we often live below those ideals because our affections are set on lesser things. Remember the simple equation:

Declared Values – Demonstrated Values = Hypocrisy

Here are some regular steps to assess your demonstrated values:

1.   What dominates your thoughts? What do you really spend most of your time thinking about? Write these down.

2.   Where do you spend your time? Spending time is spending life. If your time is spent on things that do not reflect your declared values, dissonance will result. Write down the things that consume your time each day.

3. How do you spend your money? Where your treasure is, there will your heart be also (Matthew 6:21). Honestly write down what your checkbook register reveals about your values.

4. How do you react to negative experiences in life? Review what we said about reactions in this chapter. What do your reactions reveal about the values that motivate you?

5. What would a brutally honest friend or associate say about your demonstrated values? Imagine his or her answers. Or, if you are really ready for a reality check, just ask yourself: "What demonstrated values does he or she see in my life that may be negative, destructive, or contradictory in comparison to my declared values?"

6. In a spirit of humble dependence on God, seek His grace to deal with the problems you have demonstrating your values. Use this as a time to reaffirm your declared values and to trust God for the power to live accordingly.

Question 5

"What should I do?"

*Whatever failures I have known, whatever errors I have com-
mitted, whatever follies I have witnessed in private and public
life have been the consequence of action without thought.*
Bernard Baruch[1]

*A life in which anything goes will ultimately be
a life in which nothing goes.*
John Maxwell[2]

I've heard it said many times that the two most difficult things for anyone to do are "To think" and "To do things in order of their importance." I can relate to that, can't you?

My brother, Dennis, used to have a big sign hanging over his desk during his high school days. (I was in preschool at the time and am amazed that I still remember this). In bold black letters, on a white background, it read T-H-I-N-K. Needful, isn't it? To think, to judge or consider, to be or become mentally aware or, as the prophet Haggai said, to consider our ways (Haggai 1:5, 7).

Thinking about "not thinking"

As a kid, I occasionally did stupid things. Actually, it was more often than that. For instance, we had a pool in our backyard during my early years in Albuquerque, New Mexico. It sure was fun, but it was always getting me in trouble. Correction: I was always getting myself into trouble in connection with the pool. (Self-honesty.)

One afternoon a friend and I decided to test the strength of some blocks atop a small wall next to the pool. The wall was about three feet high with these nice flat, square stones cemented all across the top. They were great for sitting on, or for lying on to sunbathe. After we managed to get the first one loose, we couldn't stop at just one. Within twenty minutes we had loosed and dumped all thirty of the stones right into the grass. When my dad discovered the results of our work he was not too happy. He asked, "Danny (my childhood name), what were you thinking?" I replied, "I don't know." His response: "Sometimes you just don't think."

Another afternoon, my parents came home to find my friends and me up to no good—again. We discovered that if we

149

climbed onto the roof of the house and got a running start and jump, we could just clear some electrical wires and land right in the deep end of the pool. Our delight was suddenly interrupted by my mother's horrified screams. How were we to know that we all could have gone to the "swimming pool in the sky" by electrocution? Again, the predictable question came, "What were you thinking?" My response, "I don't know." You guessed it. Mom reminded me, "Danny, sometimes you just don't think."

One other such memory involved an exchange with by brother, Dennis. He was about seventeen, I was six. I was in the pool having a blast, swimming by myself. Suddenly he appeared at the back door and said, "Danny, get out of the pool, the preacher is here." Our pastor had dropped by unexpectedly. Etiquette demanded that I dry off and come in to show my respect. Not wanting to leave the pool so suddenly, I responded with an obscenity. I had no idea what it meant, I just remembered a friend saying it a few times at moments like that. Before I knew it, my very angry brother had me inside, forcing me to take a bite out of a bar of Lava soap. This was apparently some kind of Baptist ritual for making a defiled mouth ceremonially clean. Once I had thoroughly chewed up this gritty tidbit (and spat it out), my brother asked me, "What were you thinking?" You know the rest of the story.

Thirty years have passed since those days in and around the pool. I now go by "Daniel." Only my dear wife can call me "Danny" and get away with it. I no longer pry blocks loose, jump off roofs, or chew on Lava soap. But every once in awhile I catch myself saying to myself, "Danny, what were you thinking?" As much as I hate to admit it, it is still true that sometimes I just don't think. How about you?

Regardless of our stage in life, we never outgrow the need to stop and think; to consider our ways—and then to do things in the order of their importance.

Too busy "doing" to "think" about doing

One business writer has described our thoughtless ways as an "urgency addiction."[3] He identifies this tendency as the habit of finding our security in busyness. The "adrenaline rush" of hurrying off to handle "important" tasks provides an artificial sense of worth, power, control, and accomplishment. But over time, our real problems worsen, relationships suffer, and we find ourselves unfulfilled, without a firm foundation.

I admit that a sense of urgency taps me on the shoulder every so often. I want to be like Joshua and pray to have God stop the sun for twenty-four hours to finish a task (Joshua 10:1–15). With those precious moments I would think deeply about these seven questions and challenge others to do the same. I would gather everyone around me and say, "All right now, pencil, paper, Bible. In the time that we have, we're going to get on our knees and start asking, thinking about, and answering these questions: *Who is God? Who are you? Why are you here? What really matters to you, and what are you going to do about it?*

The age-old addiction

Being urgency-addicted isn't anything new. The story about two sisters, Martha and Mary, gives us an opportunity to hear Jesus address the problem. It happened when Martha, distracted by all her preparations for their houseguests, asked Jesus, "Lord, do You not care that my sister has left me to do all the serving alone? Then tell her to help me" (Luke 10:40). Jesus replied, "Martha, Martha, you are worried and bothered about so many things; but only a few things are necessary, really only one, for Mary has chosen the good part, which shall not be taken away from her" (Luke 10:41–42). Where was Mary? She was seated at Jesus' feet, listening to Him.

Did one sister make a bad choice and the other make a good one? No, both made good choices. Martha, by nature, was a doer. She was an activist, who seemed to have the gift of hospitality. When she heard that Jesus was coming, she rolled out the red carpet and set about to serve Him. On the other hand, Mary was the quiet type, the contemplative one, and the one who chose to sit at His feet. She made the best choice. Sometimes a good choice is the archenemy of the best. When we take the time to stop and think before we make a choice, it makes a difference. To think deeply about what is the best choice may keep us from just running off in the direction of what is merely good.

The priorities of these women brought about two different results. Martha began to question Jesus about His concern for her, and then she told Him what He should do about the situation. This is a natural response for people whose priorities are out of order.

Frustration and complaints arise when people have their priorities out of line. "Oh, life's so hard, so tough. It's my kids, my schedule, my stress, my headaches." The emphasis is on me, me, me. Of course, Martha did remember to mention her sister. She deliberately criticized Mary's decision because she didn't, like Martha, choose to stay in the kitchen. Frustration, questioning God, and a critical spirit are some results of having wrong priorities.

What about Mary? Quiet as a mouse. She didn't defend herself or criticize her sister in return. She, apparently undaunted, just stayed at her Lord's feet. She was focused. She had her priorities straight, knew what she was doing, and displayed the peaceful result. Perhaps she exhibited the fruit of deliberate forethought about the best things.

Judging from the response Martha received, Jesus didn't speak to the preparations being made. Instead, He spoke of her attitude and demeanor. Being "worried and bothered about so many things" describes many of us, at one time or another. Jesus told Martha, "only a few things are necessary, really only one." One priority? Yes, and Mary had chosen it.

Martha made her choice, but, as Jesus said, Mary chose "the good part," which was the best. We're talking about something of lasting importance. Jesus added that what Mary had chosen would "not be taken away from her." It's a choice that will last for eternity.

These two sisters represent all of us: people with real struggles, making real choices every day. "What shall I do?" is a question evenly balanced between thinking and doing. First, wisely decide, then incorporate the decision into lifestyle.

Guarding and guiding our priorities

After thinking about and making choices comes the problem of having the discipline to do the things that matter most. I define *priorities* as the commitments we put first in our lives because we believe they are important.

The key term here is *commitments*. This word is distinguished from *prioritizing*, which is a simple function of time-management and daily tasks. Instead, we are addressing the basic areas of one's life-focus—the commitments to which we dedicate large portions of our time. These commitments ultimately determine our goals and the way we spend our time.

Some years ago, a newspaper headline told about three hundred whales that died after becoming marooned in a bay. They became trapped while pursuing sardines. One commentator observed, "The small fish lured the giants to their death. They came to their violent demise by chasing small ends, by prostituting vast powers for insignificant goals."[4]

How often have we done this! Our behavior is like the whales' in that the vast power of God's Spirit in the lives of believers is often prostituted when we chase things that are ultimately insignificant. If only we would think and do things that are ultimately important.

Lack of integration:
priorities are displaced by unimportant things

The problem with priorities is not "out there." It's not the boss, family, our schedule, or any other person. The priority issue begins inside each one of us; then, if successful, becomes visible through our daily actions. I believe we face three major obstacles that keep our priorities from coming to fruition in our lives.

The first is when unimportant things displace priorities. In his business- and life-management classic, *The Seven Habits of Highly Effective People*, Steven Covey challenges us to organize around our priorities. He suggests four quadrants. The two vertical columns are titled "urgent" and "non-urgent," while the horizontal rows are labeled "important" and "not important." He urges us to place all of our major activities in one of these four squares. The idea is to separate the "important/urgent" from the "not important/non-urgent." Ideally, we need to give more energy to the "important/non-urgent" because the "important/urgent" category typically gets the attention it requires. It's the insistent "not important/not urgent" square that must be restrained.

This picture of prioritizing our commitments raises a paramount question. What is the criterion for determining things that are really "important"? Without a solid foundation of truth our determinations may be skewed by subjectivity. We may reflect the conviction expressed by the sign on one businessman's desk: "My decision is maybe, and that's final."

Perhaps you live life as one writer described it: "If you're going to pull decisions out of a hat, make sure you're wearing the right hat."[5] If we fail to integrate our priorities with a philosophy of life that is based upon a mission, which is based upon our identity, which is based upon our theology, then we're just pulling our priorities out of a hat. It's been said that "a man can't go anywhere while he's straddling a fence."[6] We cannot afford to straddle the fence on these foundational issues so crucial to our strategic daily renewal. To do so will prevent us from going anywhere as far as doing things in the order of their importance. But, when all of these are integrated, the unimportant will rarely displace the important.

Lack of preparation:
priorities are displaced by urgent things

A second obstacle to be aware of is an internal lack of preparation. This is where priorities are displaced by seemingly urgent things. Former President Eisenhower has been credited with saying, "The urgent is seldom important, and the important is seldom urgent."

This was brought home in a tragic way when Eastern Airlines flight 401 crashed between New York and Miami. As the crew prepared to land, they noticed that a light, which indicated the landing gear was down, had failed to respond. They weren't sure if the problem was the light or the landing gear. The flight engineer attempted to remove the bulb, but it wouldn't loosen. Other members of the crew tried to help him. As they struggled with the bulb, no one noticed that the plane was losing altitude. It crashed into a swamp and people died. This experienced crew of highly trained technicians and pilots became preoccupied with an inexpensive lightbulb and a plane full of passengers became tragic casualties.[7]

All of us are on a lifetime trip. If we don't take time to prepare our hearts and thoughts according to an integrated foundation of truth, we will constantly be displacing things that matter with the inexpensive lightbulbs of life.

Lack of conviction:
priorities are displaced by unplanned things

The third obstacle to watch for is a lack of conviction. This is where the unplanned things displace priorities. We may have gotten as far as clarifying our priorities. We may have endeavored to integrate these into our lifestyles, but if we lack conviction, the internal decisions will never see the light of day.

Unplanned obstacles usually come in the form of people. One of the key leaders in my church is well known for reminding the rest of us that, "no" is a Christian word. Sometimes you have to say it, because well-meaning people who may be living in a crisis mode, are prone to request that you change your plans to fulfill theirs. But, as someone has said, "A lack of planning on your part does not constitute a emergency on my part."

This is like the old lighthouse keeper, who worked on a rocky stretch of coastline. Every month he would receive a new supply of oil to keep the light burning. Because he was near the shore, he had frequent guests. One night, a woman came from a nearby village and begged for some oil to keep her family warm. Another time, a father asked for some to use in his lamp. Someone else needed oil to lubricate a wheel.

All of these requests sounded legitimate, so the lighthouse keeper granted the requests. Toward the end of the month, he noticed that his supply of oil was very low. Soon it was gone, and the beacon went out. That night, several ships were wrecked and lives were lost. When the authorities investigated, the man was very repentant. Yet, through all his excuses and pleading, the investigators told him, "You were given oil for one purpose: to keep the light burning."[8] This was their conviction. It had failed to be his.

God has given us a theology, an identity, a purpose, and a philosophy for a reason: They help us identify the priorities that matter to Him. We need to strengthen our conviction to live for Him, even when other people may not understand our "no." Their crises will usually seem very important, yet even these will require decisions based upon strong convictions.

An example of personal priorities in ministry

As a pastor, I often have to draw upon a strong conviction about what I should be doing when responding to personal requests or expectations. In a humorous way, the following thoughts, entitled "The Perfect Preacher," pretty well covers it.

"Results of a computerized survey indicate that the perfect pastor preaches exactly fifteen minutes. He condemns sin, but never embarrasses anyone. He works from 8:00 A.M. until midnight and is also the janitor.

"He makes sixty dollars a week, wears good clothes, drives a new car, and gives fifty dollars a week to the poor. He is twenty-eight years old, has been preaching for twenty-five years, is wonderfully gentle and handsome, loves to work with teenagers, and spends countless hours with senior citizens. He makes fifteen calls daily on parish families, shut-ins, and hospital patients, and is always in his office when needed.

"If your pastor does not measure up, simply send this letter to six other parishes that are tired of their pastors too. Then bundle up your pastor and send him to the church on the top of the list. In one week you will have received 1,643 pastors. One of them should be perfect."[9]

One person, even if he were a perfect pastor, cannot do it all. Each of us should know why he chooses to do what he does.

The endeavor to live out externally the priorities that I have decided internally has caused me to clarify *five priorities* in my own ministry. I want to be what God wants me to be and do what God wants me to do. It may not be what others think I should be doing, but as long as it is my conviction to please God, I seek to *maintain, master, model, multiply,* and *mobilize* within these clarified decisions.

I am seeking to *maintain an exemplary life* (Acts 20:28; 1 Corinthians 11:1; Philippians 4:9; 1 Timothy 3:2–7; 4:12, 16; Titus 2:7–8; 1 Peter 5:3). This has to be first; without it, my credibility and ministry will fail.

Second, I seek to *master the study of God's Word* (Acts 6:2; 1 Timothy 4:6, 13–15; 5:17; 2 Timothy 4:1–2). This is another biblical imperative that no one can do for me, and ultimately results in a depth of life that makes my message authentic. Although I know about many pre-planned sermon sources, the Word must be real to me, something that flows through my life. Attached to my office computer is a sign with the words of Ezekiel 3:10: "Son of dust, let all my words sink deep into your own heart first. Listen to them carefully for yourself" (TLB).

Another one of my priorities is to *model a commitment to prayer* (Mark 1:35; Luke 6:12, 9:28, 11:1, 22:39; Acts 1:14; 6:4; Romans 15:30; Colossians 1:3; 4:2). A pastor has an obligation to lead by example. If he wants the congregation to bleed, then he must hemorrhage. Sure, anyone else can pray, but no one else can be me, and I seek to be a pastor who models prayer.

A fourth priority is to *multiply leadership within the church* (John 17:6–20; Acts 10:17–48; Ephesians 4:11–12; 2 Timothy 2:2). Leaders don't fall off trees. Spiritual leadership requires training and discipling. Future leaders need equipping that includes proper motivation, a truth-based philosophy of ministry, and a commitment to integrity.

Last, but not least, my priority is to *mobilize the church toward mission* (Matthew 28:18–20; Mark 16:15; John 20:21; Philippians 3:12–17; 2 Timothy 4:5–8). This is why we are here, and in concert with the elders, this is our chosen direction.

Because I seek to live out these internal priorities, I sometimes need to use that Christian word, *no*. When deciding my daily schedule, my internal decisions provide a firm foundation for time-management priorities.

A most profitable lesson

Charles Schwab, when president of Bethlehem Steel, asked I.V. Lee to help him with some time-management decisions. He wanted this consultant to advise him on how "to get more things done with my time." The agreement was to pay Lee anything, within reason, for his advice.

In a short time, Lee delivered a note that read something like this: "Write down the most important tasks you have to do tomorrow. Number them in order of importance. When you arrive in the morning, begin at once with number one and stay on it until it is completed. Re-check your priorities and then begin with number two, then with number three. Make this a habit.

"Every working day, pass it on to those under you. Try it as long as you like, then send me your check for what you think it's worth." In just five years, this one idea helped turn Bethlehem Steel into the biggest independent steel producer in the world. And how much did Schwab pay his consultant? Several weeks later, after receiving the note, he sent Lee a check for $25,000. He said it was the most profitable lesson he'd ever learned.[10]

This approach obviously worked when it came to ordering daily tasks. Certainly it is an important consideration when determining life commitments that reflect our values, purpose, identity, and theology.

One point should be made before we proceed with selecting priorities. This exercise needs to be executed on a yearly, quarterly, or monthly basis because the deeper the process, the more dynamic the issues become. Our theology usually will not change drastically, except as our understanding of truth grows. Identity, once based on truth, will remain intact. So will our purposes. Occasionally our guiding principles may need to be adjusted. However, because of the dynamic nature of our priorities, it is wise to evaluate them on a regular basis.

Determining priorities: six guideposts

For some, this numbering or alphabetizing of priorities is nothing new. The following question may be: What determines whether you make something 1-2-3 or A-B-C? We're walking around the edge of the philosophy camp again. It's a good place to begin the trail of life, because the forest of decisions can become very dark and dense. Here are six guideposts to watch for:

1. *Scripture*

The ultimate guidepost is Scripture: "Oh, that my steps might be steady, keeping to the course you set; Then I'd never have any regrets in comparing my life with your counsel" (Psalm 119:5–6, *The Message*). The Word of God must determine our A-B-Cs. When truth is our guide, we avoid regrets.

What is God's counsel? Well, the bulk of His counsel about priorities is found in this passage, " 'You shall love the Lord your God with all your heart, and with all your soul, and with all your mind.' This is the great and foremost commandment. And a second is like it, 'You shall love your neighbor as yourself.' On these two commandments depend the whole Law and the Prophets" (Matthew 22:37–40).

Is this counsel guiding your priority choices? Is your life, first and foremost, motivated by love? When love is the motive, then relationships are the means through which these priorities are expressed. Jesus says that the first priorities in life are relational. First, your relationship with God, then with family, friends, and others.

Dying people never say that they wish they had spent more time at the office. What really matters is relationships. Jesus makes it clear. This is "A," this is "B," then everything else falls behind these priorities.

2. *Stewardship*

The second guidepost is stewardship. The apostle Peter said, "As each one has received a special gift, employ it in serving one another, as good stewards of the manifold grace of God" (1 Peter 4:10).

Likewise, Paul said, "It is required of stewards that one be found trustworthy" (1 Corinthians 4:2). Every member, by the grace of God, has been equipped to minister. It may help to ask: "What can only I do, versus what others can do?" The answer will influence your life-management decisions.

Business writers offer this advice: "Get into the habit of asking yourself if someone else can handle what you're doing." A clear-thinking person lets go so that others can do some of the tasks that are perhaps being neglected. They will do them well; and probably better. It's one of the benefits of teamwork.

Teamwork is certainly necessary, not only in business, but in ministry. It may be risky to allow another person to fulfill someone's request, because it can result in disappointment. I know that I often disappoint people in our church. I don't want to, but I have to if I am going to live by my priorities. It's what counselors call "setting boundaries." At the end of this chapter is a chart that I have found useful in evaluating commitments.

With a church membership of approximately two thousand people, as well as hundreds of other attendees, I have come to realize that I can't keep everyone's "hope alive" when it comes to how I spend my life. Recently someone expressed a concern about my lack of priority in not attending every funeral. I understood, and tried to address this problem.

As the Lord would have it, that afternoon a staff member officiated at a funeral in our church. It was Friday, my day off, and my boys were expecting me to pick them up from school and spend some precious time together. I called the spouse of the deceased that morning to express our love and sympathy. But, instead of being at the funeral, I was with my boys—guilt-free. Why?

Long ago, I learned that twenty years from now I may be just a framed photo in the church lobby. People who know me will recognize the picture, while children will run by thinking, *Who's that old guy?* Some new pastor will be leading the ministry, proving that I was indeed expendable. But twenty years from now, I will still be the only father my children have ever known. No one else in the whole world can fill that role for them. I have a unique stewardship in being their father. This realization is enough to help me choose priorities.

3. *Servanthood*

The third guidepost is servanthood. Jesus said, "Whoever wishes to be first among you shall be slave of all. For even the Son of Man did not come to be served, but to serve, and to give His life a ransom for many" (Mark 10:44–45).

What priorities would be of most benefit to the people I am called to serve? Of all the choices, what will best serve my family? What will best serve the body of Christ? Sometimes I have to consider not only individuals, but also the whole gathering.

In my ministry, one of my priorities is to protect significant and uninterrupted study time. For the sake of the entire flock, this is essential to my primary duties of preaching and leadership. Occasionally someone will drift into the offices on a study day and can't understand why I don't take the time to chat. But to do so would be to violate, for the sake of one inquirer, my stewardship to an entire congregation. Of course, in crisis situations I make exceptions. We all must come to terms with how we can best order our lives to benefit those we are called to serve.

4. *Significance*

Another guidepost is significance. What priorities will matter in eternity? Which will mostly benefit God's work and have the greatest impact on God's kingdom? The apostle Paul said, "We look not at the things which are seen, but at the things which are not seen; for the things which are seen are temporal, but the things which are not seen are eternal" (2 Corinthians 4:18). Are my life priorities based on the seen or the unseen? Which is really significant?

In his book, *Man in the Mirror*, Patrick Morley addresses the issue of significance. He writes, "We need look no further than our own neighborhood on a Saturday morning to see how many different priorities men have set for themselves. One man rises early, while another sleeps until ten o'clock. One man plays golf every week; another watches his son's soccer game."

Giving many more examples, he continues, "Perhaps no other time of the week reveals more about us than how we spend Saturday morning. We discharge our work Monday through Friday, and Sunday is the Lord's Day, but Saturday is the day we decide for ourselves."[11]

Morley is right. Our priorities determine how we spend our time and demonstrate what we consider significant.

Paul, in his second letter to Timothy, wrote "I have fought the good fight, I have finished the course, I have kept the faith; in the future there is laid up for me the crown of righteousness, which the Lord, the righteous Judge, will award to me on that day; and not only to me, but also to all who have loved His appearing" (2 Timothy 4:7–8). Here is a man who ran the course of life with his choices based on the unseen. One may rightly conclude that his life was very significant while he lived, and remains so today as well.

Our priorities determine how we spend our time and demonstrate what we consider significant.

Clearly the Bible teaches that this visible world is passing away. If a person makes choices based upon this fading world's input, then the results are not going to last. Rest and relaxation offer an important balance in life, but soaking up sunshine in and of itself does not accomplish much that counts in eternity. On the other hand, certain vacation choices in sunny places can be a great time for ministry.

5. *Satisfaction*

The fifth guidepost is satisfaction. Jesus said to his disciples, "My food is to do the will of Him who sent Me, and to accomplish His work" (John 4:34). Is a tanned body really the key to fulfillment? Or is it knowing that your life has mattered to someone else? Yes, there is always a beach ministry, if that is what you are called to do. A beach ministry is important when it's based upon God's calling. The goal, when all is said and done, is the personal satisfaction of knowing your choice is pleasing to God.

6. *Stability*

Lastly, is the guidepost of stability. We're talking about balance again. Our lives consist of balancing many things in a limited amount of time. We must consider job, family, service, sleep, and leisure, to name just a few. And let's not forget eating. Jesus didn't. After an intense period of ministry, He said to His disciples, " 'Come away by yourselves to a lonely place and rest a while.' (For there were many people coming and going, and they did not even have time to eat.)" (Mark 6:31). Jesus helped His disciples keep their priorities straight.

Many of us have seen lion trainers at the circus. They always have whips and often a gun. I've never seen one without a stool. I've wondered if they think that little stool is going to have any deterring affect on that large lion when they point the legs toward the growling beast.

Well, those who seem to know say that the animal tries to focus on all four legs at once. This results in a kind of paralysis that overwhelms the large cat and it becomes tame, weak, and disabled. All because its attention is fragmented. Any stool legs in your life? As one writer says, "The reason most goals are not achieved is that we spend our time doing second things first."[12] The second thing becomes a first, the eighth thing moves up to third and the hundredth priority is done before the fourth. Watch out for those stool legs.

Priority choices make all the difference

The power of a single-focused life is a power that the world is waiting to see through the lives of believers. If you adequately answer the question "What shall I do?" you will stop chasing minnows into the bay like a hungry whale. Little fish lose their appeal when one sees that Scripture clearly states that part of personal identity is found in being a steward and a servant. This results in significance and satisfaction, which in turn leads to a stable, well-rounded life.

C. S. Lewis said, "If you put first things first, the second things will get thrown in. But if you put second things first, then you lose both first and second."[13] If you put the first thing first, the second will come. Jesus said, "Seek first His kingdom and His righteousness; and all these things shall be added to you" (Matthew 6:33). Now here is a life-management method that really brings some lasting results. It's sad to see that many people who claim to be Christians fail to follow this time-tested approach. As a consequence, life ends in a bay, like a beached whale surrounded by deceptive minnows.

Robert Frost wrote a classic poem about these tragic types of decisions. He talked about choosing between two roads, a choice facing a person walking in the woods. This wanderer would like to explore both roads since they seem equally inviting. However, as he contemplates the decision to be made, he realizes that he must make a choice. Frost describes the scene this way:

> *Two roads diverged in a yellow wood,*
> *And sorry I could not travel both*
> *And be one traveler, long I stood*
> *And looked down one as far as I could*
> *To see where it bent in the undergrowth;*
>
> *Then took the other, as just as fair,*
> *And having perhaps the better claim,*

Because it was grassy and wanted wear;
Though as for that, the passing there
Had worn them really about the same,

And both that morning equally lay
In leaves no step had trodden black.
Oh, I kept the first for another day!
Yet knowing how way leads onto way,
I doubted if I should ever come back.

I shall be telling this with a sigh
Somewhere ages and ages hence:
Two roads diverged in a wood, and I—
I took the one less traveled by,
and that has made all the difference.[14]

The moral of this pilgrim poem is that any life choice between alternatives that often appear to be equally attractive will bring, as years pass, far different results. Every day brings many roads to travel. The question will always be, "What should I do?" Hopefully, the answer will be based on Scripture, stewardship, servanthood, significance, satisfaction, and stability.

Join me in an honest recommitment to consider carefully the things that really matter. Sign up now, as well as in the tomorrows of your life, in order to reap the rewards of strategic daily renewal. And, may it be that we will never have to look our Lord in the face on that day when His pleasure will be all that matters, and hear Him say, "What were you thinking?"

A personal guide to developing your priorities

We have defined *priorities* as the commitments we put first because we believe they are important.

It is important to clarify the commitments that are most important. You cannot do everything but certainly you ought do the best things.

The table on page 168 lists the six guideposts described in this chapter. (Review the descriptions as needed.) Across the top you will see four key areas of your life where priorities often need to be clarified. Use this chart to help you start establishing priorities. Or, make your own chart to complete this vital exercise.

This is a brainstorming activity. You may put a lot of ideas in the various boxes. After you have filled in this chart, take time to review, synthesize, and organize your ideas. The net result will be a list of the priorities you will want to commit yourself to keep straight.

Be sure to write these conclusions in your life-planner or somewhere else where you keep your other key statements. Review your priorities regularly.

This is an exercise that should be done at least once every year to make certain that you are integrating your priorities with the other vital issues in your life.

Remember, these commitments are based on your values, purpose, identity, and theology. Review the components of your foundation for your priorities often.

	Personal	Family	Work	Ministry
Scripture: What does the Bible say are the commitments that matter most?				
Stewardship: What can only I do? What commitments best utilize my "S-DNA"?				
Servanthood: What commitments will best meet the real needs of those I am called to serve?				
Significance: What commitments will advance God's kingdom and matter most in eternity?				
Satisfaction: What commitments will be most rewarding based on my foundations?				
Stability: What commitments will bring balance and well-being over the long haul?				

Question 6

"How should I do it?"

*The world stands aside to let anyone pass
who knows where he is going.*
David Starr Gordon[1]

*Give me a stock clerk with a goal
and I will give you a man who will make history.
Give me a man without a goal
and I will give you a stock clerk.*
J. C. Penney[2]

*Be not afraid of going slowly;
be only afraid of standing still.*
Chinese proverb

The New Testament often compares the Christian life to a contest, or, more specifically, to a race. Paul talks about fighting, working, and straining with purpose, direction, and discipline. And in the twelfth chapter of Hebrews, the writer stresses that the victorious runner is the one who lays aside everything that hinders.

I remember running track in junior high and high school. No matter how much I ran, the conditioning was always grueling. We often ran to the point of total exhaustion. Before each season began, we would start conditioning and strengthening our muscles by running with leg weights. Of course, we would never think of wearing the weights during a track meet; we laid them aside. By comparison, when living the Christian life, we're not practicing. We cannot afford the encumbrance of weights in this race.

The writer of Hebrews also says that the runner's eye must be fixed on the goal. He was referring to a runner in the Olympic Games, whose eye is fixed on a square pillar located at the finish of the race. For every Christian, the writer maintains, the goal is Jesus.

Paul often used the example of running. In Galatians he said that he wanted to run in a way that would not be vain or meaningless. In Philippians 3, he focused on running and finishing the race to win the prize that God promised him, the high call of Jesus Christ. And in his second letter to Timothy, he mentioned the Lord's promise of a wreath, or a crown, for the winner who keeps the rules of the contest.

But in Philippians 3, Paul may have been referring to a chariot race. In New Testament times, these races were held in many cities of the Roman Empire. Paul pictured himself as a charioteer who, in a decisive moment of the race, strained forward to what lay ahead. Intensely pressing toward the goal of the prize, at a high speed, Paul noted that even one glance backward could be tragic and, perhaps, even fatal in this race. For him, Christians must forget what they've achieved in the past and must, with newly bestowed grace, strain forward with all their might.

In these races, judges would sit by the goal, carefully prepared to render their final decision. In Paul's letter to Timothy, he wrote, "There is laid up for me the crown of righteousness, which the Lord, the righteous Judge, will award me in that day; and not only to me, but also to all who have loved His appearing" (2 Timothy 4:8). This kind of race and reward demands our all.

Paul's ultimate long-range life goal was to become like Christ and finish the ministry that God had given him. Along the way Paul established many short-term objectives, plans, and goals.

Writers of today's business literature sometimes overuse the word *goals*. This word is sometimes repulsive to Christians; they may perceive it as unbiblical. That is understandable, but perhaps somewhat reactionary. It may help to establish a working definition of this term.

An explanation of goals

This word originally meant "pole, rod, or stick." Historically, *goal* has meant something visible that would be positioned at the end of a race course so that all participants could keep their eyes on this stick. The word is used to signify an object that has been set as a finishing point.

In Greek, the word is *scopos*, from which we get the word *scope*. It represents a mark on which someone would fix his eyes. From these two definitions I've developed this working model: A goal is a mark toward which you plan your life so that you can accomplish your priority commitments and live with integrity.

After we clarify our priorities and come to valid conclusions about what really matters, we take the next step of establishing specific marks, or targets. It's these marks that we set our eyes on, in an all-out effort to see our priorities become reality.

Is goal-setting biblical?

Actually, the answer is yes and no. It all depends, because a goal is like a rung on a ladder. Whether the goal is good or not depends on the rest of the ladder. It depends on the focus and foundation. It depends on the ground upon which the ladder is resting and the wall against which it is leaning. Again, it may help to have some examples of bad goals versus goals focused on the glory of God.

Biblical examples of a bad approach to goals

An example of a poor goal is the Tower of Babel described in Genesis 11:4. The people basically said, "We want to build a tower and a city so that we can reach heaven and make a name for ourselves." In response to their goals, God scattered them and gave them different languages. He had put within them the potential of imagination, creativity, and teamwork; yet they had chosen a bad goal.

A goal is a mark toward which you plan your life so that you can accomplish your priority commitments and live with integrity.

*

Another example is the self-sufficient king in Jeremiah 22:13–14. He purposed to build a large and impressive dwelling in a manner that took advantage of his neighbors by not paying them for their work. The goal was bad and the results were worse.

Then there's King Nebuchadnezzar in Daniel 4:28–36. One day, this king was on the rooftop of his palace, looking at his great kingdom. He thought, *Look what I have done in building this residence by my power and for my glory.* God, in effect, said, "Bad goal, Nebuchadnezzar," and this king found himself acting like an animal, with long hair and fingernails, eating grass in the field. This continued until he learned how to choose good goals, instead of bad ones.

The New Testament has numerous examples of bad goals as well. One is the rich fool of Luke 12. He must have had too much time on his hands and was looking for something to do. He decided to tear down his old barns and build bigger ones for storing all his goods and wealth. Then he could say to his soul, "Eat, drink, and be merry." In response to this goal, God declared the king a fool. He said, in effect, "You're poor toward Me. You may be rich, but your goals and thoughts are way off base. The ladder you're climbing is on the wrong foundation, and it's propped against the wrong wall."

Another example is the businessman in James 4: "Come now, you who say, 'Today or tomorrow, we shall go to such and such a city, and spend a year there and engage in business and make a profit.' Yet you do not know what your life will be like tomorrow. You are just a vapor that appears for a little while and then vanishes away. Instead, you ought to say, 'If the Lord wills, we shall live and also do this or that.' But as it is, you boast in your arrogance; all such boasting is evil. Therefore, to one who knows the right thing to do, and does not do it, to him it is sin" (4:13–17).

Now these people had appropriate short-term plans. They also had planned long-term for the next year. They had a city in mind, and a particular objective of making money. James didn't say their goals were bad. He said, "You ought to say, 'If the Lord wills . . . .' " He also pointed out that they were planning out of arrogance, self-will, and selfish desire. The problem, in this and other examples, is not that they had goals. The complication comes when the goal is motivated by a wrong heart and finite objective.

God acknowledges that man will have many plans, "but the counsel of the LORD, it will stand" (Proverbs 19:21). Plans are not wrong. Many people in the Bible had plans, but remember this: It is only the counsel of the Lord that will stand. And that brings us to some examples of good goals.

Biblical examples of a good approach to goals

We'll start in the Old Testament with Noah's goal of building an ark. God gave Noah a plan. The dimensions were specific, measurable, and attainable. Of course, the task was formidable, yet Noah set about to faithfully obey. God gave him a time frame and the reason behind the project. Noah understood that God was going to establish His righteousness on earth and He was going to do it specifically through Noah and the ark.

God was also very specific in telling Moses to build the tabernacle. The instructions included the materials, the people, the timing, and more. With Joshua, entering the Promised Land, God gave specific goals, city by city. Solomon, when given the vision of building the temple, received very specific instructions.

In the book of Nehemiah, God gave the long-term goal of rebuilding the wall of Jerusalem. In response, Nehemiah made this goal the priority of his life. He began this task by accomplishing short-term goals. First, he had to get permission from the king. He became accountable by telling the king that, if granted permission, he planned to do it in a certain amount of time. Then he began to survey and plan, to find the right people, to provide motivation, and to deal with opposition. Nehemiah is a wonderful example of setting goals—the right kind.

In the New Testament, the best example of good goal-setting is Jesus Christ. Even though the Bible is not specific, we can learn valuable lessons from His life. At the end of Jesus' ministry He prayed, "I glorified Thee on the earth, having accomplished the work which Thou hast given Me to do" (John 17:4). Jesus never lost His commitment to the goals and plans that fulfilled His mission.

Take the wilderness experience, for example. He didn't just go for a walk and then decide to stay for forty days and not eat. No, this was by design. It was a specific step toward a mark. So too was His baptism by John.

And what about the selection of the twelve disciples? Why not ten or eighteen? Because there was a plan, formed in ages past. Specific events needed to occur. These events had a design, a timetable, an order, and an objective.

Jesus went to the cross at the appointed hour, He was buried according to plan, and He rose from the grave exactly three days later, just as He had predicted. All of this happened by design, to accomplish the ultimate purpose of redemption. He, being God, fulfilled many measurable segments of this long-range plan. Because we are not God, we need to plan and implement with great dependence upon His Spirit and His Word.

Paul knew this as he sought guidance for his life, actions, and travel plans. He wrote, "Often I have planned to come to you (and have been prevented thus far) in order that I might obtain some fruit among you also. . ." (Romans 1:13). Paul had plans, but he also had dependence upon God. In verse 10, he said, "Always in my prayers making request, if perhaps now at last by the will of God I may succeed . . . ."

The process of establishing goals

With these examples in mind, let's move to the actual process of establishing goals. The biblical analogy of a race works well as a framework. Blending experiences of running

track with the scriptural picture of a race, we will look at six
steps in the goal-setting process:

1. Consecration
2. Preparation
3. Imagination
4. Execution
5. Evaluation
6. Celebration.

Step one: consecration

A successful track season, and effective completion of each
race, begins with consecration. To run with excellence, you
must decide on absolute commitment to the season and its rig-
ors. This means setting aside any distractions and hindrances
that are not consistent with top conditioning.

Every year during track season, my lifestyle changed as I
traded junk food for the healthy stuff. Instead of late-night
goofing off, I was careful to get adequate rest. I traded afternoon television for healthy workouts. This took consecration
and commitment.

A consecrated perspective

When it comes to goals, we must continually give our hearts
to God and discard meaningless and temporal ambitions. We
must submit our plans to the Lord to confirm that our goals are
the same as His.

Not all goals are God-given and people can become very
temporal when the time comes for serious goal-setting. When I
was in college, I read some information about life-planning and
was motivated to write three pages of goals. Over the years, I
have misplaced those pages, but I do remember a few of my
intentions. A major one was to own a herd of buffalo by the time
I was thirty. Now is that a God-given goal? I think not, but I've
always been intrigued by this great American animal, so I
thought that this would be a good thing to pursue. Of course, at

that stage in life I did not understand that goals should be integrated with a biblical foundation for life.

We often miss the mark when it comes to what our goals should be. I recently read a speculative account describing the day Jesus took His disciples up to a mountain to teach some aspects of the Sermon on the Mount. "Blessed are the meek, blessed are those who mourn, blessed are the merciful, blessed are you when you are persecuted," He instructed. "Blessed are you when you suffer. Be glad and rejoice for great is your reward in heaven." In this scene, Simon Peter asked, "Are we supposed to know this?" Andrew said, "Do we have to write this down?" James wanted to know if they were going to be tested on the material. Philip didn't have any paper, and on it goes with the other disciples. Then, one of the Pharisees, asking to see the lesson plan, inquired, "Where is your set of anticipatory goals and objectives in the cognitive domain?" The scene closes with these words, "And Jesus wept."

Sometimes we get so wrapped up in tangible, temporal things. We really don't understand the biblical perspective of goals, so we dash off to round up a herd of buffalo. Goals can be biblical. God wants us to make commitments that are specific, accountable, and measurable, in fulfilling His will.

Consecrated plans

We may have great thoughts about who God is and who we are in Christ. We can have answers based on truth as to why we are here, what we really believe, and what we should do. This is all very motivating. But now, the question is: "What are we going to do about it?" How will we get there? We're talking about goals and commitment.

As one person said, "There is one elementary truth, . . . at the moment one definitely commits oneself, then Providence moves too. All sorts of things occur to help one that would otherwise never have occurred, a whole stream of events issue from the decision, raising in one's favor all manner of unforeseen incidents and meetings and material assistance which no man could have dreamt would have come his way."

As a college student, my hope was to become a pastor and to serve the Lord. Then I decided that a good priority would be to plant a church. That's when the pressure started. Specifically, a small group of us decided to plant a church in the Pacific Northwest. This added a little more pressure. Then we decided we were going to do it by a certain time, and this resulted in a greater consecration. But, as we established those goals, dates, and specific strategies, God moved and provided in unbelievable ways.

We were fresh out of seminary and didn't know what we were doing when we moved two large trucks full of furniture, nine cars, three babies, five married couples, four singles, and fifty thousand dollars across the country toward the Pacific Northwest. We hadn't won the lottery, but people saw that we had specific goals and they believed in our vision and commitment.

This very first ministry experience became an amazing illustration of the power of specific commitment. God showed Himself strong on behalf of those who, based upon the call of God, were willing to act in specific ways. That is what Paul referred to when he spoke of intensity, commitment, and urgency.

Six factors in consecrating our plans

Another dimension of consecration is the importance of submitting plans to the Lord on a continual basis. Patrick Morley beautifully describes this process in his comments on Proverbs 16:1–4.

> The plans of the heart belong to man,
> But the answer of the tongue is from the Lord.
> All the ways of a man are clean in his own sight,
> But the Lord weighs the motives.
> Commit your works to the Lord,
> And your plans will be established.
> The Lord has made everything for its own purpose . . . .
> (Proverbs 16:1–4).

"Six essentials," he says, "are contained in this passage, with the first being found in the beginning sentence, 'The plans of the heart belong to man . . . .' " First, I should tell God what my goals are. This is when I verbalize my plans and my goals to Him.

The second element is found in the idea "the answer of the tongue is from the LORD." Here is where I listen to what He has to say. I'm often surprised by His response. I mean, "You're not into buffalo, Lord? This isn't such a good idea?"

The third phase is where it says, "All the ways of a man are clean in his own sight . . . ." This is when I try to convince God to let me do it anyway. You know the conversation: "Now, Lord, you just don't understand. This is a good thing. Buffalo must be in your plan for me!" Step three is usually where I engage in a little debate.

The fourth key is found in the truth that "the LORD weighs the motives." Here is where God lets me know that He sees through my argument. His response leads me to the next discovery.

"Commit your works to the LORD, and your plans will be established." This fifth step is where I humble and empty myself, and listen. "Okay, Lord, I will trust you and the plans you have for me." And this is not just a feeling. It's a commitment where I say, "There it is. It's all yours. I'm emptying myself of my herd of buffaloes, and tuning in to your counsel."

The final truth is found in "The LORD has made everything for its own purpose . . . ."[3] This is where God gives me His goals for my life. What an exchange! I trade my buffaloes for something that has tremendous, amazing, eternal significance. His plans for me will bring fulfillment and instruction on how to progress toward the goal of ministry and Christlikeness that He's designed for me.

Step two: preparation

A second major step in the process of establishing goals is preparation. In running track, it's the issue of making certain you are ready for the race. How's my energy? Have I warmed up sufficiently? Am I mentally prepared? Is my equipment in good shape? Do I fully understand the distance or duration of this contest?

Preparing effective goals

To prepare for establishing goals, we must understand the nature of good goals. When these dynamics are understood, we are ready to become specific.

For a goal to be effective, it should be specific, measurable, and attainable. How does one become specific in setting goals? Sometimes it helps to have an example of what specific doesn't look like. "Well, I'd like to be healthy" is a priority, not a goal. To move toward this priority, the goal would be to push that dinner plate away from you five minutes earlier. Or, to stop eating a breakfast of bacon, eggs, ham, biscuits, and gravy. To do these two things, for a specific amount of time, is a goal.

Specific goals can be short- and long-range. Paul's daily goal was to become renewed and to continue his ministry. His long-range goal was to finish the race. Between these goals were the specific towns, cities, and areas where he sought to minister.

Effective goals are also measurable. Written goals can be evaluated in a tangible way. They have time lines and deadlines. This is the difference between a goal and a wish.

A good goal helps a person to be accountable. It's also one reason that many people shy away from goal-setting. By establishing a standard of measurement, we become answerable as to whether or not we are making progress. In counseling, one method is to give the client a homework assignment of some goal to be accomplished by the next appointment. Whether or not the person follows through says some major things about the original problem. Most of us prefer to live in the twilight of non-accountability.

Attainability is another aspect of an effective goal. We are talking about the reasonable hope of crossing a finish line. This is why short-term goals are an integral part of long-term goals. As we meet each short-term goal, we become increasingly hopeful of reaching the distant target. The idea is to stretch toward accomplishments that we know are reasonable, decent, worthwhile, and attainable.

It helps to think of goals as stepping-stones to accomplish the plans God has placed upon one's heart. Too many times, good intentions settle down on the clouds of aspiration, instead of marching forward on goal-accomplishing stepping-stones. Many people say, "I'd like to do this," "If only . . . ," and "I wish . . . ." These are soft clouds of aspiration. Such people have many ideas and desires, but no accomplishment. The difference between clouds and stepping-stones is a commitment to clear, pre-determined, God-given goals. To know this is to be prepared for worthwhile goals.

Step three: imagination

Every runner thinks ahead and rehearses the race before it begins. He envisions his start out of the blocks, imagines the turns of the track, and dreams of a solid finish.

The holy use of the imagination is an important function. It enables us to understand the accomplishment of the goal through the eyes of faith. This hopeful expectation of accomplishment helps us as we prepare to act upon those things God has placed upon our hearts.

A few years ago, Karl Walenda, the famous tightrope artist, died after falling from a rigging tied seventy-five feet above the ground.

His wife, who was also an aerialist, had an interesting observation about his actions before the fatal fall. She said, "All Karl thought about for three straight months was trying not to fall. He kept thinking about falling. It was the first time he'd ever thought about that, and it seemed to me that he'd put all his energies into not falling, rather than in walking the tightrope." She added that her husband went as far as to personally supervise the installation of that particular tightrope, making absolutely certain the guy-wires were secure. Before, he'd always trusted his crew to do this.[4]

We need to trust God. Our focus should not be on failing, but on the vision He has for our lives. The reality of what He can do should keep us steady on the tightrope of life.

The final regular season game for the San Francisco 49ers in 1997 was in Seattle, Washington, against the Seattle Seahawks. San Francisco boasted of the best record in the league and was headed to the playoffs with home field advantage. Seattle was finishing a mediocre year. The game meant nothing to the 49ers but was an exciting challenge for the Seahawks. As you might guess, the better team lost. In interviews with the coach afterward it was clear that the 49ers' goal was simply to keep the players from getting hurt. With that attitude, even extraordinary teams will lose. The only way to win is to stay focused on the goal of winning. Any lesser objective spells disaster.

When Noah had a goal, he could build an ark that offered salvation from the flood. When he lost his vision, he got drunk. Saul's goal was to conquer kings. He lost his focus and couldn't conquer his own jealousy of David. When David imagined God's power at work, he conquered Goliath. When he lost his faith, he couldn't conquer his own lust. Solomon had goals and hopeful expectations of being the wisest man in the world. When he lost what God had given him, he couldn't control his own obsession for foreign women. When Samson had a clear focus, he won many battles, yet when he lost it, he failed to win his battle with Delilah. Elijah's goal was to pray down fire from heaven. It ended when he ran in despair from Jezebel. The apostle Peter pledged himself to the death for Christ when his faith was foremost. Yet, he denied Christ altogether before a mere servant girl when he lost sight of his Lord.

It is the hopeful imagination, the sense that God is doing something, that gives direction for our energies. Good goals motivate us to keep going, in faith. God is constantly stretching us forward to new targets, to new marks of doing His will. The question is, are you doing it?

Step four: execution

When the starting gun goes off, every ounce of your being must be committed to the effort of the race. The same thing happens in the execution of good goals, when you carefully and prayerfully write them down. Execution is an everyday kind of thing. Keep these easily available as they are a key component in your daily time of personal spiritual renewal. They become building blocks to a life where everything fits together. I have found this to be essential.

Step five: evaluation

In a race, evaluation is essential. This is done with split-second analysis, and it is key to a good finish. You examine your pace, stay in your designated lane, monitor your breathing, adjust your posture, and, straining forward with all your energy, you also focus on the finish line.

When implementing a goal, evaluate the following: Am I staying focused? What distractions and hindrances do I need to be aware of? What are my time deadlines and how am I doing in meeting these? All during this procedure, pray about these things, commit them to God, and trust Him for the grace to arrive at the worthwhile finish line.

It's best to double-check and confirm that your understanding of God's plan is based on the right foundation. One man explains it this way: "High achievers nowadays talk a lot about goal setting. But they sometimes seem to talk as if it doesn't really matter *what* goals we have, as long as we have goals. Targets to shoot at. Dreams to pursue. Any target. Any dream. But not all goals are created equal."[5]

He goes on to say that good judgment is required when setting goals. Many people have been disappointed because, upon reaching their goals, nothing worthwhile was there. "True success," he continues, "is not just attaining goals. It is attaining goals that are worth attaining. . . . A beautiful house built on a bad foundation cannot provide for secure and stable long-term habitation."[6]

This conclusion reminds me of the wisdom Jesus shared when He said, "Everyone who hears these words of Mine, and does not act upon them, will be like a foolish man, who built his house upon the sand. And the rain descended, and the floods came, and the winds blew, and burst against that house; and it fell, and great was its fall" (Matthew 7:26–27).

Good judgment comes from prayer, the goaltender of your plans. Prayer keeps you ever-dependent on the Lord as you trust Him and receive His direction.

So how can one be sure he or she is building on the right foundation? Perhaps the following summarization can help:

TIME MANAGEMENT accomplishes GOALS
GOALS fulfill PRIORITIES
PRIORITIES implement VALUES
VALUES guide PURPOSE
PURPOSE expresses IDENTITY
IDENTITY springs from THEOLOGY
All of these are based on the truth of God's Word!

When you make it your lifetime occupation to know who God is, you will progressively understand who you are in Him. As you are able to define your mission in life, you will make wise decisions that will be the guiding principles for direction. With these in place, you'll establish priorities that really matter and make wise commitments. This leads to confidence that those specific targets, or marks, will be pleasing and glorifying to the Lord.

Step six: celebration

A final and important part of the goal process is celebration. What runner does not celebrate a well-run race? During the 1996 Summer Olympics, Michael Johnson set a new world's record in the 200 meters. As he finished the race, he glanced over his left shoulder to see the digital readout of 19.32 seconds. His jaw dropped in disbelief and he let out a lion-like roar amidst the cheering spectators. Then he dropped to his knees and he bowed his head before being swarmed by other runners who came to congratulate him. A few minutes later he ran a victory lap, stopping to hug and thank his mother and father. He knew how to celebrate the accomplishment of his goal.

God's people also knew how to celebrate. Look at the feasts, festivals, and worship services they held to commemorate their deliverance, the completion of their places of worship, and battle victories over opponents.

It's good to remember to celebrate the goals God enables us to accomplish. These become specific, measurable marks that serve as reminders that we are truly living our theology, identity, purpose, values, and priorities. They are visible milestones of God's faithfulness and grace. Even if it is a simple journal entry of thanksgiving, or a few moments of spontaneous singing—celebrate! Have some friends over and tell them how God has helped you—throw a party! Sanctify the moment!

Isn't it amazing what God has given us to carry out our God-given goals? Paul, in his letter to Timothy, encouraged the young man by reminding him of his calling, gifts, and opportunities. He reminded Timothy that the flame of potential needs to be fanned, not extinguished by a spirit of fear. Timothy had received power, love, and a sound mind. He was to build on what God had given him and carry on with the commitment. How often do we acknowledge and thank God for His power working in us?

Consider this story about one of the great mountains in the Alps. This mountain is popular with the climbers because it has a rest stop, about halfway up. If one starts at the base, the building can be reached at around lunch time.

Over the years, the owner of this rest stop has noticed an interesting phenomenon. When climbers get to this point, they feel the warmth of the fire, smell the good food, and begin to relax in the surroundings. Often, they will tell their companions to climb on without them. "We'll head back to base camp with you," they say, "on your way down."

A glazed look of contentment comes over them, as they sit by the fire, play the piano, and sing mountain-climbing songs. In the meantime, the rest of the group get their gear and trek to the top. For the next couple of hours a spirit of happiness wafts through the house. "But," the owner says, "by midafternoon, it starts to be quiet." The climbers who stayed behind begin taking turns looking out the window, staring at the top of the mountain. They're silent as they watch their friends reach the goal. The atmosphere changes from one of merriment to an almost funeral-like quietness as they realize that they forgot their commitment and settled for second-best. They missed the real celebration.[7]

The climbers who went on to reach the mountaintop not only knew they could do it, they decided they would do it. Those plans that God has put in your heart, believe them to be possible. If you're building on the right foundation, bathing your goals in prayer, building toward them with the potential God has given you, then believe it! Activate your faith by continuing on in your commitment, then remember to celebrate His faithfulness and grace when He finishes what He started.

It's never too late

It's never too late to implement biblical worthwhile goals through consecration, preparation, imagination, execution, evaluation, and celebration.

John Maxwell has noted various individuals who discovered the value of new goals even in their advanced years. People like Colonel Sanders who, at seventy years of age, originated "finger-lickin' good" chicken; and Casey Stengel who became manager of the *Yankees* baseball team at seventy-five; Picasso was still painting at eighty-eight; George Washington Carver, at eighty-one, became head of the Department of Agriculture; Thomas Edison, age eighty-five, invented the mimeograph machine; and John Wesley still traveled on horseback and preached when eighty-eight.[8] All of these people had a vision, some biblical, some not. Still, the attitude was, regardless of age, to "press on."

At whatever age, what are you willing to commit yourself to? How will you do it? When will you do it? Will it be because you know who God is? And because you know who you are in Him? And because you know why you are here, what you believe, and what really matters?

How will you do it? One day at a time, with solid consecration, thoughtful preparations, holy imagination, focused execution, careful evaluation, and joyful celebration. Commit to choose your marks not on whims, wishes, or wants, but on the will and Word of God.

A personal guide to developing good goals

Use the six steps that follow as a guide to developing good goals. You will need to make multiple copies of these pages and use one sheet for developing goals to fulfill each priority you identified in chapter 5.

My priority
Write the priority these goals will accomplish.

Rough draft

Write down the goals you will need to aim at to achieve this priority.

1.

2.

3.

4.

Step one: consecration

What areas of my life will I have to surrender to God in order to accomplish these goals?

Am I willing to make the sacrifices necessary to pursue these goals?

Read Proverbs 16:1-4 and review pages 179 and 180. Below, write out a goals-related prayer in which you surrender your heart and ambitions to God.

Step two: preparation

As you prepare to implement these goals, take time to evaluate whether they are ready to be pursued.

Are these goals specific? If so, in what way? If not, write the specifics that need clarification.

Are these goals measurable? If not, put some measuring mechanisms in place for each one. How will you know when you are on course? How will you know if your pace is on target for accomplishing these goals?

Are these goals attainable? What could keep me from attaining these goals? Is it realistic to overcome those hindrances? If not, adjust the ambition of the goal. If the hindrances can be overcome, explain how?

Step three: imagination

In what way will these goals require faith?

What positive outcomes will occur if you achieve these goals? Write these down.

What promises of God's Word will you focus on to keep your faith growing? Write them down.

When and how will I systematically pray about these targets?

Step four: execution
Having completed the first three steps, write a final version of your goals.

Step five: evaluation (Complete this step once a month.)
Are these goals still integrated and consistent with the foundations of theology, identity, purpose, values, and priorities? If not, how can you make adjustments?

Are you on target with the established measurements? If not, how can you make adjustments to stay on course?

In what ways are you regularly trusting God by faith for these goals?

Step six: celebration (To be completed just before the goals are met.)

How will you celebrate the accomplishment of these goals? When will this occur? Who will you include?

How can you give praise and thanksgiving to God for this achievement?

Question 7

"When should I do it?"

Humans live in time . . . therefore . . .
attend chiefly to two things,
to eternity itself and to . . the present.
For the present is the point at which time touches eternity . . .
in it alone freedom and actuality are offered.
C. S. Lewis[1]

When I was a child I laughed and wept—
Time crept!
When as a youth I dreamed and talked—
Time walked!
When I became a full-grown man—
Time ran.
Then with the years I older grew—
Time flew!
Soon I shall find as I travel on—
Time gone![2]

When it comes to getting a grip on time, it seems that the harder we work, the "behinder" we get. One man, when thinking about time, wrote, "We talk of no time, the lack of time, not enough time, or being out of time, trying to get more time. We borrow time only to incur a time debt and end up with even less time." He observes that the atmosphere in the workplace is so time-management conscious that skills and time-compression techniques are constantly being sought. "This sense of time urgency," he writes, "creates time pressure and time stress. Then it's crisis time."[3]

Time defined

Just what is this thing called *time*? You can ask many different people and receive a variety of answers. A dictionary defines time as "a unit of geological chronology" or "any specified or defined period." I define time as my habitual expenditure of the stewardship of life.

Now this phrase, the "habitual expenditure of the stewardship of life," may be one that you don't often hear, but the truth is that our lives are not our own. We tend to segment our understanding of time with labels like, "work time," "family time," "leisure time," "nap time," "meal time," and the like. In reality, it is all "God's time." Since it is His, we'd better be careful about what we do with it.

I remember attending a retreat where I listened to Bill Mills, president of Leadership Resources. He gave a definition of time that I will never forget. He said, "Time is the realm in which God works out in us what has already happened in His

195

heart and mind in eternity."[4] God has entrusted every person with life; time is life and life is time. Bottom line: Time speaks of the habits related to what we do with every twenty-four hour segment that God grants us for His eternal purposes.

Our habits with time

When addressing the subject of habits, one person wrote, "You may know me. I'm your constant companion. I'm your greatest helper. I'm your heaviest burden. I will push you onward or drag you down to failure. I am at your command." He says that a habit is easily managed, if you are firm and show exactly how you want it done. Then habit will do it automatically. "You may run me for profit," he continues, "or you may run me to ruin. It makes no difference. Be easy with me, and I will destroy you. Be firm with me, and I will put the world at your feet."[5] These brief comments pack a mighty punch about the expenditure of time.

Some people have good habits when it comes to spending hours, minutes, and seconds. Others have developed unhealthy practices. Most of us have a few of each. But some people's habits turn into addictions.

Once curious about addictive habits, our daughter wanted to know if an addiction was "kind of like what I have with my blankie?" She had been carrying her blanket around for a long time and confessed, "I said when I turned five I was going to give it up, but I keep asking for it every night. Is this an addiction?" Then our oldest son asked, "Is it kind of like baseball cards? The more I get, the more I want. Is this an addiction?"

Our son had baseball cards on the brain, and it could be considered an unhealthy habit for him. For me, it's sunflower seeds. Everywhere I go, I leave a few hulls behind. Compared to some addictions, blankets and baseball cards and sunflower seeds seem harmless.

Still, the most important habit, the one that can be con-
structive or destructive, revolves around our use of time. It is
not an easy habit to change. It frustrates us because the faster
we go, the "behinder" we get.

Our history with time

Frustration with time began early in man's experience.
History records a statement of a man named Plotinus who, in
200 B.C., cursed a sundial. He uttered, "The gods confound the
man who first found out how to distinguish hours! . . . who in
this place set up a sundial to cut and hack my days so
wretchedly into small portions."[6] Have you ever felt that way
about time?

Thirty years ago futurists were peering into their crystal
balls and predicting that one of the biggest problems for coming generations would be decisions concerning their abundance
of spare time. Authorities testified before a senate subcommit-
tee in 1967 that by 1985 people could be working twenty-two
hours a week or twenty-seven weeks a year, and could retire at
age thirty-eight. More than thirty years have passed since then
and maybe I've missed something. But so have many others; a
Harris survey showed that leisure time enjoyed by the average
American has decreased 37 percent since 1973. Over this same
period of time the average workweek, including commuting,
has jumped from fewer than forty-one hours to more than
forty-seven. Today, many of us would say it seems even longer
than that.[7]

"Paradoxical as it may seem," says one commentator,
"modern industrial society, in spite of an incredible prolifer-
ation of labor-saving devices, has not given people more time
to devote to their all-important spiritual tasks; it has made it
exceedingly difficult for anyone, except the most determined,
to find any time whatever for these tasks." Here is his opinion: "The amount of genuine leisure available in a society is

generally in inverse proportion to the amount of labor-saving machinery it employs."[8] In a nutshell, the more sophisticated we become, the less time we have.

In America, time seems to be our master instead of our slave. In my travels to other countries, I find that time is handled differently. It seems to be associated more with relationships, the spiritual, the family, and the soul, than to a domineering wristwatch. Whether I was in Indonesia, Romania, Jordan, or Moldova, folks always seemed to have time for a leisurely cup of tea and a friendly chat.

Ghandi once said, "There is more to life than increasing its speed."[9] We can manage faster, write faster, read more quickly, and communicate briefly. We have fast food, microwave meals, and ready-made snacks. This tendency toward rushing occurs even within the walls of some churches that boast of offering eight- to twelve-minute sermons. This helps the listener to experience God faster?

Perhaps you have read these well known words of wisdom: "I have only just a minute, only sixty seconds in it, forced upon me, can't refuse it, but it's up to me to use it. I must suffer if I lose it, give account if I abuse it, just a tiny little minute, but eternity is in it."[10] There's more to life than just increasing its speed.

The practical side of "the time of our lives"

Given the increasing sophistication of our society and our parallel struggle with limited time resources, the seminars and books on time-management will likely be around for a long time. If only we could find time to attend those workshops and read the books they might actually help us! I confess that, over the years, I have accumulated quite a collection of resources on time-management. I've read dozens of books, listened to many tape series, and attended countless seminars. They can all be helpful. But the real key is to understand time from a biblical perspective. This will be the main focus of the rest of this chapter.

Ten quick tips on time

For now let me give you a very quick summary of ten practical ideas for trying to develop some good habits in your expenditure of "the stewardship of life." This is a perspective on how to better understand and control the minutes, hours, and days of your earthly pilgrimage.

1. Realization

The Bible tells us that our life is a vapor. Not too impressive or enduring is it? We "appear" for a moment, then vanish. The older I get, the more I realize that this earthly journey is at best a brief appearance.

In the process of writing the final draft of this book, I had the privilege of traveling to Michigan to spend some time with the publishers in Grand Rapids. While there, I carved out a couple of days to be with a dear friend of mine named Steve. He lives with his wife Karen and their three delightful sons in the nearby village of Nashville. We became very close friends in college, and worked together for years to start a church in the Northwest. Our families have stayed in touch; our kids are similar ages. We have simply enjoyed much of our adult years as good friends.

I visited his church on a Sunday. He leads worship there. At the end of the service, Steve stood before the congregation to introduce me. He proudly announced that our friendship goes back thirteen years to our college days. As he continued the introduction, you could hear a low roar in the crowd. Finally someone interrupted him and said, "Steve, you mean twenty-three years, not thirteen!" Steve's reaction to this revelation was a humorous combination of shock, embarrassment, and disbelief. Somewhere along the way, he overlooked ten years of life. Even though we had noticed that a lot of his hair had turned gray and even more of my hair had turned loose, we still cannot understand how twenty-three years could have passed since those carefree college days. Life is, indeed, a brief appearance.

That's the practical reality which prompted the psalmist to pray, "Lord, make me to know my end, and what is the extent of my days. Let me know how transient I am. Thou hast made my days as handbreadths, and my lifetime as nothing in Thy sight. Surely every man at his best is a mere breath" (Psalm 39:4–5). The first practical step to time management is to realize how little of it we really have and how quickly it will run through our fingers like sand.

2. *Preparation*

It has often been said that people don't plan to fail, they just fail to plan. Every Monday I take an hour or so just to work on my schedule. Although my administrative assistant actually schedules all of my appointments, it is still my responsibility to coach her on the available time slots, based on my priorities. I think ahead to the appointments, counseling sessions, staff meetings, and sermon preparation days. I prepare my mind and heart. I pray about the week. I gather special items needed for these obligations.

The same principle applies to each day. Pausing to think for a few minutes in the morning, before rushing aimlessly out the door with the cereal bowl in your hand and your shoes untied, will save you headaches later. It has been said that ten minutes spent in planning will save at least an hour during the day. That's good stewardship.

3. *Standardization*

You can usually tell how disorganized someone is by how many different sizes and types of paper they use to write things down. That is where a standardized planning system helps immensely. Furthermore, take your calendar, hold it by the outside binding, turn it upside down, and shake it. The more little pieces of scrap paper and "loose ends" that fall out, the greater your need to work on how you keep track of life. Try to standardize your time-tracking and life-planning tools. You'll be glad you did.

4. Delegation

In a commitment to mutual effectiveness and growth, share the load with others. It is important to look through your tasks and time commitments and ask, "Is there anyone who can accomplish this as well as, or better than, I can?"

We often suffer under erroneous conclusions about the issue of delegation. We think we don't have time to delegate. In reality, we don't have time to do otherwise. We think we can do it quicker or better. Perhaps—but not in the long run. Besides, how will others learn unless we give them an opportunity? Busy mothers can employ children much more than they often do to accomplish chores around the house. In delegating, Mom gets a break while the kids learn greater responsibility and a good work ethic. I have always been delightfully surprised to witness the positive fruit of delegation. People often excel in handling delegated responsibilities, and I am free to focus on goals more significant to my unique calling.

5. Communication

Time-management is a team effort. We often forget that we are interdependent with others in what we do with our time. I have found that spending time explaining my schedule and plans with my family, staff, and friends is a great help in the long run. They give me solid and realistic feedback. I find that they are also more sensitive to the value of my time as I try to be a good steward each day.

6. Evaluation

Periodically, it is important to look back as well as ahead. While tedious, we all need to track how we have spent a day by keeping a log. Once you've done that a few times, try it for a week. Then make a serious investigation of how your activities matched your plans and accomplished your goals. Gurus on the matter of time almost universally agree on the importance of doing this at regular intervals.

7. *Elimination*

Bill Yeager, a retired pastor and friend, is noted for saying, "Every healthy body needs a good elimination system." Of course, this is true about our physical body. (He actually uses this idea in reference to churches.) This statement is also true with reference to our calendars. You can't add important obligations without removing the less important items. Again, there are only so many hours in a day. It's easier to add than to subtract. Eliminating time commitments is not always easy or popular. It is essential. Goals, priorities, values, purpose, identity, and theology will guide you in what to eliminate.

8. *Adaptation*

One of my favorite beatitudes, from the book of "Second Daniel" reads, "Blessed are the flexible, for they shall not be broken." Proverbs 16:9 says, "The mind of man plans his way, but the LORD directs his steps." Since God is the owner of our time we need to be sensitive to His leading in executing our well-laid plans. The late Oswald Sanders highlights this truth well when he says, "Few things are more apt to produce agitation and tension in a busy life than unexpected and unwelcome interruptions. To Him (Christ) there were no such things as interruptions in His God-planned life."[11]

9. *Integration*

Queen Elizabeth I, when facing imminent death, said, "All my possessions for a moment of time."[12] This is how precious time is. We need to constantly remember how important it is and respond accordingly. We must take time each day to review our "foundations for living." Time spent in reviewing the seven questions in this book, and your answers to them, will guide daily choices of time-management and add meaning to the minutes of your life. This may be the difference between spending a day of your life on earth or investing a day of your life for eternity. Whether you are in the shower, sitting in a meeting, pausing for a snack, or dozing off to sleep, the battle for integrity and significance can stand or fall on these quick and quiet minutes of focus.

Napoleon once said, "There is in the midst of every great battle ten to fifteen minutes that are crucial. Take that period and you win the battle. Lose it and you'll be defeated."[13] If we have not prepared our hearts, we may lose the battle. I find that each day brings the need for me to prepare myself for the battle of life. Time spent in answering these essential questions is the key to victory in the day-to-day stewardship of life.

"I will never do anything which I should be afraid to do if it were the last hour of my life."

10. Eternization

I had to look hard for this word. It is a real word, and it means "to make something eternal." This has to do with our time. In all things I ask myself, "What can I do in this minute or hour that will really matter in eternity?" As C. S. Lewis said, "The present is the point at which time touches eternity. . . . in it alone freedom and actuality are offered."[14]

Jonathan Edwards shared this good advice, both by his life and by his words: "I will never do anything which I should be afraid to do if it were the last hour of my life."[15] Edwards understood the importance of eternal significance.

How many people, on their deathbeds, ever requested their time-management notebooks? In these moments, his or her need is not to have someone read from the past month's calendar. Usually, they want to hear some words of wisdom and comfort from the Bible. Often they want to be near the people with whom they have made memories in the moments of life. Those final hours have a way of condensing what really matters. Why wait until then, when the opportunity is now? Sooner or later, we all come to realize that the longest life here on earth is just a breath in light of eternity.

"Just a tiny little minute, but eternity is in it." This connection between time and eternity urges us to be sure we understand time from God's perspective. To do this we turn to His Word.

The biblical perspective on time

God's Word gives us a solid understanding of the biblical concept of time. Paul wrote, "Be careful how you walk, not as unwise men, but as wise, making the most of your time, because the days are evil. So then do not be foolish, but understand what the will of the Lord is" (Ephesians 5:15–17).

When Paul said to be careful how you walk, he was not referring to your choice of shoes, or watching where you put your feet. He was speaking about life. Paul's warning can loosely be translated this way: "Observe accurately, in a spirit of investigation, as you look at your life." How you walk represents lifestyle and habits of behavior that result in the spending of your precious time. Paul cautions his readers to be wise, not foolish.

In Psalm 90:10–12, we see what wisdom looks like: "As for the days of our life, they contain seventy years, or if due to strength, eighty years, yet their pride is but labor and sorrow; for soon it is gone and we fly away. Who understands the power of Thine anger, and Thy fury, according to the fear that is due Thee? So teach us to number our days, that we may present to Thee a heart of wisdom."

The psalmist said, "Number your days." Paul said, "Be careful how you walk." Make an accounting of everything you're doing and ask, "Is what I know to be true being implemented in the habits of my behavior?"

Paul also said to make "the most of your time, because the days are evil." He was not talking about modern time-management, where the idea is to try to squeeze more seconds out of every minute. The idea here focuses on purchasing something, buying something back. Paul is saying, "Redeem the time." It's not yours automatically. You have to seize it, reach for it, and grasp it. Why? Because the days are evil.

The world's way of life will rob you. It's going to hold your time hostage unless you buy it back and take control of it, using it for God's purposes, not for evil. Someone or something is going to control your time expenditure. It will be either you or the world's beckoning call.

Chronos versus *kairos*

Let's pause for a moment to define two Greek words translated *time*. The first is *chronos*, from which we get the word "chronology." This is the idea of continuous time that is measured in hours, minutes, or seconds.

The second word for time is *kairos*, which is the idea of a fixed moment or a season of opportunity. The difference between these two words is the difference between a minute and a moment. A minute is measured by seconds on a clock. A moment is measured by an experience or an opportunity.

Treasuring the moments

A powerful and poignant illustration of the importance of "moments" versus "minutes" is seen in the way we treasure memories. When was the last time you heard someone say, "Do you remember October 14, 1996? Wasn't that twenty-four hour period truly life-changing?" Or have you ever said to anyone, "Do you remember the special memory we shared at 3:17 P.M., two years ago?"

Instead, we all recall with great fondness an event or relational encounter, not because of the date or time, but because of the meaning of the moment. Days, hours, and minutes speak powerfully to our lives only when they have become the avenues of real "moments." If we can understand the value of "moments" versus "minutes" in the past, wouldn't it be wise to do so with the present and future time that is before us?

On November 19, 1863, a consecration service was held on a blood-stained battlefield at Gettysburg, Pennsylvania. In just three days during July of that year, over 40,000 casualties were incurred in that decisive battle. The time had come to formally dedicate that final resting place.

The original keynote speaker for this solemn ceremony was a man named Edward Everett. He was an extraordinary orator with cultured words, patriotic fervor, and public popularity. As a former governor and congressman, this sixty-nine-year-old statesman was a natural choice for this momentous gathering. Through an unanticipated turn of events, the commissioners of this service also invited President Abraham Lincoln. When the commissioners learned that the president planned to attend, they asked him to offer "a few appropriate remarks" as well.

When the day came, Edward Everett rose to give his speech according to plan. His memorized oratory flowed with masterful fluctuation and dramatic gestures. Everyone, including President Lincoln, was captured with his eloquence. Finally, an hour and fifty-seven minutes later, Everett concluded with the crowd applauding enthusiastically.

A short while later, President Lincoln was introduced. His notes consisted of two simple handwritten pages, with thoughts borne out of his own great burden and tears over the wartime situation of the country he led and loved. With very little gesturing, but deep personal passion, he delivered his own Gettysburg Address. In two minutes he was finished.[16]

Almost one hundred and forty years have passed since that day of solemn remembrance. No one can recall one line from the two-hour speech of the orator. Yet, Lincoln's two minutes of passion—flowing from deep conviction and clear purpose—are among the most memorable thoughts in the history of our nation. This illustrates the difference between minutes and moments.

Seizing the moments

Paul did not use *chronos* when he said to make the most of our time. He did not urge us to control our hours and minutes or to fill in our daily and weekly schedules. He was not talking about a time-management system. He was talking about buying back the moments, not the minutes.

We are dealing with *kairos*, the opportunities that God brings across your path. Paul, in effect, said, "You've got to aggressively buy this time back or you're going to miss the God-given moment." Capture them, seize them, and buy them back from a world that is stealing them away!

Think of the people in Noah's day who missed a pivotal moment in time. Another moment was missed, as we read in Luke 19, when Jesus entered Jerusalem and walked among the people. They also failed to grasp this important opportunity. How did Jesus respond? He wept.

I remember the first sermon I ever preached. I used this passage and I called it "Must Jesus Weep Again?" For some, this is a serious question. Will Jesus, along with us, weep over the lost opportunities of our lives? We can lose an opportunity for service, an opportunity to say "yes" to an occasion of ministry. One can, perhaps at this very moment, grasp the opportunity for knowing Christ, accept Him for who He claims to be, and receive what He is willing to give. The offer of eternal life, through salvation in Jesus Christ, is an opportune moment that no one should fail to redeem.

Biblical time-management

Biblical time-management is not so much a matter of controlling the calendar, but of capitalizing on the opportunities. The time-keeping program on my computer is not the principle Paul was talking about. Nor would Paul's priority be served by those time-management systems that many people faithfully fill out and carry around.

Any number of books and seminars can teach you the fine art of making lists, ordering tasks, handling interruptions, dealing with paperwork, and staying on top of phone messages. This chapter is about understanding, anticipating, and maximizing the "moments" of your life—an often overlooked and ultimately important issue of time-management.

An ancient Greek statue depicts a man with wings on his feet and a large lock of hair on the front of his head. He has no hair on the back of his head. Beneath this statue is the following inscription:

> Who made thee? Lysippus made me.
> What is thy name? My name is opportunity.
> Why hast thou wings on thy feet? That I may fly away
>   swiftly.
> Why hast thou a great forelock? That men may seize me
>   when I come.
> Why art thou bald in back? That when I am gone none can
>   lay hold of me.[17]

This is what Paul meant. Opportunity has wings on its feet and it must be seized in advance, as it comes, as it's here. Once it is gone, the possibility of grasping it is gone. Control your time from this biblical time-management wisdom. Instead of mastering your calendar, become a master of your opportunities.

Time-management wisdom is summed up in these words: "Do not be foolish, but understand what the will of the Lord is" (Ephesians 5:17). And how does one understand? Understanding the "will of the Lord" as it pertains to time is to face our days based on the foundation of theology, identity, purpose, values, priorities, and goals.

This means walking in dependence upon Him, being filled with the Spirit of God. When we do, He gives us understanding, wisdom, and insight into the truth of God. This enables us to see the time, seize the time, and become wise stewards of the habits of our daily lives.

An example of the proper use of time

Only Jesus could be the perfect example. He lived with a perfect heart of understanding. He said that He came "not to do My own will, but the will of Him who sent Me" (John 6:38). Along with this understanding was a sense of urgency. In John 9:4, we read Jesus' words, "We must work the works of Him who sent Me, as long as it is day; night is coming, when no man can work." The foundation of understanding time is seen in the importance and needfulness of doing God's will.

Christ's firm grasp of opportunity

As we continue to learn from Jesus' example, we see Him ministering with a firm grasp on opportunity. In John 7, all Jews were going to Jerusalem to celebrate the Feast of the Tabernacles. Jesus saw this opportunity, not from the standpoint of when the Feast began *(chronos)*, but from the understanding that this was the time to accomplish God's purpose *(kairos)*. Members of His family were pushing for Him to immediately go and prove Himself publicly, yet He replied, "Go up to the feast yourselves; I do not go up to this feast because My time has not yet fully come" (John 7:8). *Chronos* time may have come for the Feast, but *kairos* opportunity was not yet there. God-given opportunity does not always happen according to a clock, but according to the moment of eternal significance.

Even in the hour of His crucifixion, Jesus was obediently aware of the passing moments. He said, "For this purpose I came to this hour" (John 12:27). Later we read that Jesus knew "His hour had come that He should depart out of this world to the Father" (13:1). This is our example of wise time-management, a pattern to follow when making habitual decisions.

Christ's perfect display of wisdom

When it came to His limited time on earth, Jesus showed perfect wisdom. This was particularly true in two areas: renewal and reproduction. In Matthew 14, Jesus received some very heavy and troubling news. His dear cousin and forerunner, John the Baptist had just been beheaded. When He heard this, "He withdrew from there in a boat to a lonely place by Himself" (14:13). The multitude followed Him. Without any sign of resentment or stress, He fed these thousands with five loaves and two fish. After the masses had left, he returned again to the priority of getting away "by Himself to pray" (14:23). This was a regular part of His "habitual expenditure of the stewardship of life" (as confirmed in Mark 1:35 and Luke 22:39). What wisdom for those who wish to find a pattern for the wise use of time!

He also knew the wisdom of habitually investing His time reproducing His character and life in those who would carry the torch to the next generation. As he drew closer to the time of His death, He spent increasing amounts of time with the inner team of disciples. The fruit of this investment was seen in the Garden of Gethsemane, just before Jesus was to die, when He prayed to His Father. He said, "I glorified Thee on the earth, having accomplished the work which Thou has given Me to do . . . . I manifested Thy name to the men whom Thou gavest Me out of the world; thine they were, and Thou gavest them to Me, and they have kept Thy word" (John 17:4–5). He was the perfect model of what it means to "redeem the time" with true wisdom.

Finding kairos *in the chaos of* chronos

Most of our planning, when it comes to time, deals with the "minutes" of life instead of the "moments." However, biblical emphasis is almost the opposite. Yet this does not mean we should neglect structure and organization. After all, "God is not the author of confusion" (1 Corinthians 14:33). What it does show is that we have not understood the value of time until we firmly grasp, actively anticipate, and purposefully pursue the moments God places before us. We can learn to "seize the moments" not just "spend the minutes."

In planning *kairos* in the chaos of our *chronos*, we first realize that moments can always be found in the midst of our chaotic schedules. And they are chaotic. It's said that the average American is interrupted seventy-three times a day. For an average manager, it's an interruption every eight minutes. We receive 600 advertising messages every day and travel an average of 7,700 miles every year. In that same year, we watch 1,700 hours of television. We spend six months of our lives waiting for traffic lights to change, and one year searching for misplaced objects. We spend another eight months opening junk mail, two years calling people who don't answer or whose line is busy, five years waiting in lines, and three years in meetings.[18] With the invention of the Internet, you can add to this thousands of hours in a lifetime answering e-mail and surfing the information superhighway.

With such a pace, it's comforting to know that while moments and minutes are distinctive and may often have to be handled separately, in the course of a day we can choose to make a moment out of any minute and buy back the time.

Eternal moments with your eternal God

Speaking of decisions, wise time-management includes the decision to capture moments for personal renewal. All of this talk about making wise choices, changing bad habits for good

ones, and incorporating truth into lifestyle can be overwhelming at the outset. As we've already seen—Jesus, even in His
perfection, understood the necessity of spending time in the
Father's presence. His habit was to rise early and to find a
solitary place in which to pray. Because of this practice, He
was enabled to minister effectively when opportunities
occurred.

Most of us are impatient with the things of God, because
we don't have or take time for God. We fail to buy back these
precious moments. Consequently, we fail to minister in His
wisdom, will, and Spirit. We lose opportunities and don't use
time to its full advantage. Time for daily renewal brings us
into the *kairos* mode so we can see the "moments" of life more
clearly.

The Living Bible paraphrases Proverbs 10:27 in this
manner: "Reverence for God adds hours to each day."
Significant periods of renewal and reflection are one of the
most powerful tools for true biblical time management. Jesus
knew the value of time alone in the wilderness. The early
church pursued extended days of prayer. Biblical examples
show us that many of the great personalities sought extensive
amounts of time for renewal. They knew they must "come
apart" before they "came apart."

This is vital to true integrity. If you are to integrate your
time usage with your theology it is vital to spend time with the
God of your theological foundation. He is also the God of your
new self, your purposes, values, priorities, and goals.
Maintaining and cherishing spiritual renewal will make all the
difference.

Eternal moments for eternal souls

One of the most important things is remembering to be
open to the people who enter into your daily life. Are you
ready and willing to make an eternal impact on them or is your

day so tightly scheduled that God-given purpose is forgotten? Wise time-management includes being open to the spontaneous work of the Holy Spirit.

Every seemingly mundane minute, when spent with another person, carries the potential of a *kairos* moment of eternally significant impact. It's been said that "time, wisely used, gives relationships top priority." A lunch appointment can be a moment of sharing the good news of Jesus Christ with the waiter or waitress. The usual meeting at work can close with a moment of impact as you speak a caring word or genuine compliment. We are told to conduct ourselves wisely, "making the most of the opportunity. Let your speech always be with grace, seasoned, as it were, with salt, so that you may know how you should respond to each person" (Colossians 4:5–6).

Instead of just taking your children to the dentist, plan to talk on the way about principles that matter. On the return trip, stop for ice cream. Between licks, remind them of how important they are to you and why. This turns a menial trip into a meaningful moment.

Another way of making the most of your time, from an eternal perspective, is to learn how to bring the presence of God, and your dependence on Him, into the minutes of your day. When driving, instead of listening to the radio, spend trip time praying. Pray about your life. Pray for open doors of ministry. Pray for your family. Pray for the people in the cars around you and see the masses as Jesus sees them, with compassion rather than frustration. This is called "praying on site, with insight." It can be done anywhere and at any time. Necessary errands become encounters with eternity, and minutes turn into moments.

These are examples of living in the wisdom of an eternal perspective. Proverbs 9 says, "I, Wisdom, will make the hours of your day more profitable and years for your life more fruitful." While modern time-management tools tell us how to get more done with minutes, God's wisdom (seeing life from an eternal perspective) tells us how to get more life into our moments.

Numbering our fleeting days

I'll never forget an article that spoke to my heart about time, and the limited amount of it we have left here on earth. The writer begins by mentioning a family game called *Boggle*. This game contains several cubes with a single letter on each side. The challenge is to take randomly organized rows and, within a time limit, see who can form the most words.

"Sometimes," he writes, "the configuration of letters is such that a seemingly limitless number of words can be formed. In those games, I invariably get caught off-guard when somebody calls out, 'Time's up!' It seems we were just getting started! We all knew there was a time limit; we just didn't expect the game to end so soon!

"Such was the feeling that I had several months ago when a dear friend of our family was fatally injured in an automobile accident. We all know that there's a divinely determined time limit to our lives here on this earth, but somehow, I just wasn't prepared when I received word that David was medically brain-dead, followed by the news one week later that his heart had finally stopped beating.

"From a human vantage point," he continues, "there were a number of reasons why those who knew David and loved him were shocked by the news of his death. David was a strong, healthy twenty-two-year-old college student. He was generous, big-hearted, and had a seemingly infinite capacity to love people. He was in school preparing for a lifetime of ministry. The possibilities of this dedicated young man's future seemed limitless. So it was natural to feel that the "timer" on David's life had run out too soon.

"Yet we know that the timer on each of our lives is held and controlled by the righteous, wise hand of our loving heavenly Father. . . .Through David's death, those of us who loved him have had to enter into a deeper level of trust in a God who does not make mistakes and who measures out for each of us a predetermined number of days in this mortal flesh.

"But," he continues, "there is another message that has gripped my heart in the wake of David's homegoing. And that is the fact that we have no guarantee about tomorrow. It is so easy to presume upon the future. 'Tomorrow I'll get serious about spiritual growth . . . .' 'When I finish this project, I'll start spending more time with my wife and kids . . . .' 'One of these days I'll make restitution for that item I stole . . . .' 'Someday I'll seek forgiveness from the parent I rebelled against . . . .' And on and on we go, living in the world of tomorrow. The only problem is, tomorrow may never come.

"As he pondered the eternality of God's existence and the brevity of man's existence, Moses cried out to God, 'So teach us to number our days, that we may apply our hearts unto wisdom' (Psalm 90:12 KJV). You see, not until we agree with God that our days are numbered will we set our hearts to seriously pursue wisdom. And what is wisdom?

"True wisdom," he says, "is the ability to look at every detail throughout each day of my life from God's point of view. God alone knows how many days each of us will have to seek Him and to obey His truth. According to Psalm 90, God grants us about seventy years on the average. Seventy years—just 25,550 days. I have already spent over 14,000 of those days. If God is gracious, I may have another 11,000 days or so in which to glorify and please Him.

"But there is no guarantee that I will be given many days," he writes. "God gave my friend, David, only 8,267 days. God gave His only Son 12,000 days in which to accomplish His plan on this earth. However, as the moment approached when the 'timer' on His life would be finished, Jesus was able to say, 'I have glorified thee on the earth; I have finished the work which thou gavest me to do' (John 17:4 KJV).

"For every one of us, at the end of our days there will come a time when we must give account of how we invested those days. Unfortunately, when God calls, 'Time's up!', many of us will be caught off-guard. We may want to protest, 'But I was just getting started!' Then with shame we will have to confess that our days were spent pursuing our own pleasure and goals, and that, while we gave lip service to the lordship of Jesus Christ, in reality we lived for ourselves."

In his final paragraph he says this: "We can only speculate about when God's 'timer' for our lives will run out. But, by His grace, we can determine to live our lives with the conscious realization that life, at best, is short, and therefore we must 'apply our heart unto wisdom.' We can dedicate each day He gives to us to glorify Him and to fulfilling His perfect will, while we still have breath."

And then this is his final line: "So, Lord, teach us to number our days."[19]

Del Fehsenfeld, Jr., the writer of this article, was the founder and leader of a ministry called Life Action. Based on the date of this article, just eight hundred and fifty days later, he learned that he was dying of brain cancer. Two hundred and thirty-five days after that, he stepped into eternity, leaving his wife and family of five children. In the article he had written that he might have 11,000 more days in addition to the 14,000 he'd already spent. Instead, he lived only slightly more than 1,000.

That, my friend, is why the issue of "When should I do it?" is one of the seven most important questions you will ever ask. The time to ask is today, not tomorrow, or next week. If God has touched your heart, seize the moment now.

He was going to be all that a mortal could be . . .
No one should be kinder nor braver than he . . .
Tomorrow;

A friend who was troubled and weary he knew
Who'd be glad for a lift and who needed it, too;
On him he would call and see what he could do . . .
Tomorrow.

Each morning he stacked up the letters he'd write . . .
And thought of the folks he would fill with delight . . .
Tomorrow;

It was too bad, indeed, he was busy today,
And hadn't a minute to stop on his way;
"More time I'll have to give others," he'd say . . .
"Tomorrow."

The greatest of workers this man would have been . . .
The world would have know him had he ever seen . . .
Tomorrow;

But the fact is he died, and he faded from view,
And all that he left here when living was through
Was a mountain of things he intended to do . . .
Tomorrow.

Anonymous

Today is the day to begin a biblical, habitual expenditure of the stewardship of life through strategic daily renewal.

A personal guide to a healthy, habitual expenditure of time

The worksheet below is designed to be used at the beginning of every week as you construct and/or evaluate your schedule.

Step one: evaluating the minutes *(chronos)*

Take time to look at your schedule using the ten quick tips. Note any adjustments you need to make or items for which you need to plan. Also note any insights you gain about your week as you prayerfully complete this exercise.

Quick Tip	Insights/Adjustments/Plans
Realization: Take a few minutes to see this week as but a vapor. Ask God for wisdom to number your days as you should this week.	
Preparation: When will you take time each day to pre-pare yourself for the day's schedule and gather any necessary resources?	
Standardization: How can you standardize paperwork and other tools of time-management this week? Get rid of loose ends and scraps that clutter your life.	
Delegation: Are there any items on your schedule that you should assign or share with someone else? Take time to give them clear instruction and authority.	
Communication: With whom do you need to share your schedule and plans? As nec-essary, make copies of your calendar; phone these peo-ple, or sit down with them.	

Quick Tip	Insights/Adjustments/Plans
Evaluation: When did you last keep a log of your activities and actual schedule? When will you do this next? Will you do it this week? If so, prepare the materials.	
Elimination: Is there any regular activity that you need to stop doing? Is there anything on this week's schedule that needs to be dropped? Who must be informed?	
Adaptation: What activities might be interrupted? Yield to the Lord on these items. Consider in prayer how you will handle unexpected disruptions.	
Integration: Have you thoroughly reviewed the six foundations for your time? How does your schedule implement these principles? How can you better integrate?	
Eternization: What are you doing that is eternally significant? How can you make your activities more significant in light of eternity?	

Step two: experiencing the moments(*kairos*)

Column one below lists the days of the week. Columns two, three, and four identify areas in which *kairos* often occurs. In these columns, note the minutes that could become moments. Note the sample.

Day	Renewal	Reproduction	Ministry
Tuesday (Sample) Other opportunities to look for: • pray with people on the phone • pray through newspaper as I read about events	<u>In shower</u> (5:30 a.m.)—review memory verses, sing praises; <u>Exercise with wife</u> (7:00 p.m.)—prayer walk/pray for neighbors	<u>Staff meeting</u> (9:00 a.m.)—share a leadership principle; <u>Lunch with John</u> (noon)—challenge him with a vision to start a new ministry	<u>Driving kids to school</u> (7:30 a.m.)—read 1 John 1 together; <u>Gas station</u> (5:15 p.m.)—Ask attendant about prayer requests for his family
Sunday Other notes:			
Monday Other notes:			
Tuesday Other notes:			

Day	Renewal	Reproduction	Ministry
Wednesday Other notes:			
Thursday Other notes:			
Friday Other notes:			
Saturday Other notes:			

Epilogue

The great thing is to be found at one's post as a child of God,
living each day as though it were our last,
but planning as though our world might last a hundred years.
C. S. Lewis[1]

Rejoice, O young man, in your youth,
And let your heart cheer you in the days of your youth;
Walk in the ways of your heart,
And in the sight of your eyes;
But know that for all these
God will bring you into judgment.
Therefore remove sorrow from your heart,
And put away evil from your flesh,
For childhood and youth are vanity.
Remember now your Creator in the days of your youth,
Before the difficult days come,
And the years draw near when you say,
"I have no pleasure in them."
Ecclesiastes 11:9–12:1

I want to close with a story that emphasizes the importance of taking time to ask yourself these seven most important questions. After reading it, you will understand why it is important to do this now, rather than later. It's called, "The Little Old Man."

"You're going to meet an old man someday down the road—ten, thirty, fifty years from now—waiting there for you. You'll be catching up with him.

"What kind of old man are you going to meet? That's a rather significant question. He may be a seasoned, soft, gracious fellow, a gentleman who has grown old gracefully, surrounded by hosts of friends, friends who call him blessed because of what his life has meant to them. Or he may be a bitter, disillusioned, dried-up old buzzard without a good word for anyone; soured, friendless, and alone.

"The kind of old man you will meet depends entirely on yourself," says the writer, "because that old man will be you. He'll be the composite of everything you do, say, and think, today and tomorrow. His mind will be set in a mold you have made by your beliefs. His heart will be turning out what you've been putting into it. Every little thought, every deed goes into this old man. He'll be exactly what you make of him. It's up to you. You'll have no one else to credit or to blame.

"Every day and in every way you are becoming more and more like yourself. Amazing, but it's true. You're beginning to look more like yourself, think more like yourself, talk more like yourself. You're becoming yourself more and more. Live only in terms of what you're getting out of life, and the old man gets smaller, drier, harder, crabbier, more self-centered. Open your life to others, think in terms of what you can give, your contribution to life, and the old man grows larger, softer, kindlier, greater.

"The point to remember is that these things don't always show immediately. But they'll show up sooner than you think. Those little things so unimportant now—beliefs, attitudes, ambi-

225

tions—they're adding up inside where you can't see them, crystallizing your heart and your mind, and someday they'll harden into that old man. Nothing will be able to soften or change them.

"The time to take care of that old man is right now. Today. This week. Examine his values, his motives, his attitudes. Check up on him. Work him over while he's still plastic, still in a formative condition, because the day comes awfully soon when it's too late. The hardness sets in worse than paralysis. Character crystallizes, sets and jells. That's the finish.

"Any wise businessman takes inventory regularly. But his merchandise isn't half as important as he is. Better take a bit of personal inventory. We all need it, and by keeping this check on ourselves, we'll be much more likely to meet a splendid old fellow at the proper time. The kind of fellow any of us would like to be."[2]

This same wisdom has been expressed before, but in fewer words: "Do not be deceived, God is not mocked; for whatever a man sows, this he will also reap" (Galatians 6:7).

As we come to the concluding moments in our consideration of *The Seven Most Important Questions You Will Ever Answer,* our real journey begins.

I sincerely hope some significant seeds of truth have been planted deep within the soil of your heart. Theology. Identity. Purpose. Values. Priorities. Goals. Time. May they bring forth the fruit of a life well lived so at the end of your earthly travels, you'll find yourself completely ready to step through the doorway of eternity.

My prayer for you, my friend, is the same as was Paul's hope for the Colossian believers. I pray you will be filled with the knowledge of His will in all spiritual wisdom and understanding, so that you may walk in a manner worthy of the Lord, to please Him in all respects, bearing fruit in every good work and increasing in the knowledge of God.

May God in His infinite patience and grace bring forth these pearls of truth in the days that are before you.

Appendix 1

The Attributes of God

Eternal - God has no beginning, and He is not confined to the finiteness of time or of man's reckoning of time. He is, in fact, the cause of time. (Deuteronomy 32:40; Isaiah 57:15; Revelation 1:8)

Faithful - God is always true to His promises. He can never draw back from His promises of blessing or of judgment. Since He cannot lie, He is totally steadfast to what He has spoken. (Deuteronomy 7:9; Psalm 146:6; 2 Timothy 2:13)

Good - This attribute of God causes Him to give to others in a way which has no motive and is not limited by what the recipients deserve. (2 Chronicles 5:13; Psalm 106:1; Nahum 1:7)

Gracious - Our God is a forgiving God. His goodness and compassion cause Him to not treat us as our sins deserve; but instead to provide the way for our salvation. (Nehemiah 9:31; Isaiah 30:18; 2 Corinthians 9:8; Ephesians 1:6)

Holy - God is a morally excellent, perfect being. His is purity of being in every aspect. (Leviticus 19:2; Isaiah 47:4, 57:15; 1 Peter 1:15)

Immutable - God is always the same in His nature, His character, and His will. He never changes, and He can never be made to change. (Numbers 23:19; Psalm 102:25–27; Malachi 3:6; Hebrews 13:8)

Impartial - The Lord of the universe does not show favoritism nor partiality. He does not treat any one of us as our sins deserve, but freely offers His grace to all. (Deuteronomy 10:17; Job 34:19; Romans 10:12; 1 Peter 1:17)

Incomprehensible - Because God is God, He is beyond the understanding of man. His ways, character, and acts are higher than ours. We only understand as He chooses to reveal. (Job 11:7; Isaiah 55:8-9; Romans 11:33)

Infinite - The realm of God has no limits or bounds whatsoever. (1 Kings 8:27; Psalm 145:3)

Jealous - God is unwilling to share His glory with any other creature or give up His redeemed people. His holiness does not tolerate competitors or those who sin against Him. (Exodus 20:5; 34:14; Joshua 24:19)

Just - In all of His actions, God acts with fairness. Whether He deals with man, angels, or demons, He acts in total equity by rewarding righteousness and punishing sin. Since He knows all, every decree is absolutely just. (Numbers 14:18; Psalm 89:14; Romans 3:25–26)

Longsuffering - God's righteous anger is slow to be kindled against those who fail to listen to His warnings or to obey His instructions. The eternal longing for the highest good for His creatures holds back His holy justice. (Exodus 34:6–7; Psalm 78:38; 2 Peter 3:9)

Loving - The attribute of God which causes Him to give Himself for another, even to the laying down of His own life. This attribute causes Him to desire for the other's highest good without any thought for Himself. This love is not based upon the worth, response, or merit of the object being loved. (1 Chronicles 16:34; Jeremiah 31:3; Romans 5:8; 1 John 4:7–11)

Merciful - God is an actively compassionate being. In His actions, He responds in a compassionate way toward those who have oppressed His will in their pursuit of their own way. (Deuteronomy 4:31; Psalm 62:12, Micah 7:18; Romans 9:14–16)

Omnipotent - God possesses all power. He is able to bring into being anything that He has decided to do, with or without the use of any means. (Genesis 18:14; Job 42:2; Jeremiah 32:27; Ephesians 3:20–21)

Omnipresent - God is present everywhere, in all the universe, at all times, in the totality of His character. (Psalm 139:7–10; Proverbs 15:3; Jeremiah 23:23–24; Hebrews 4:13)

Omniscient - God knows all. He has a perfect knowledge of everything that is past, present, or future. (Job 37:16; Psalm 139:1–6; Proverbs 5:21; Romans 11:33)

Righteous - God is always good. It is essential to His character. He always does the right thing. Ultimately, since He is God, whatever He does is right. He is the absolute. His actions are always consistent with His character, which is love. (Deuteronomy 32:4; Psalm 119:142; Hosea 14:9; Matthew 5:48)

Self-existent - There is nothing upon which God depends for His existence except Himself. The whole basis of His existence is within Himself. There was a time when there was nothing but God Himself. He added nothing to Himself by creation. (Exodus 3:14; John 5:26)

Sovereign - God is totally, supremely, and preeminently over all His Creation. There is not a person or thing that is not under His control and foreknown plan. (Job 9:12; Psalm 99:1; Daniel 4:35; Acts 4:24–28)

Transcendent - God is above His creation, and He would exist if there were no creation. His existence is totally apart from His creatures or creation. (Isaiah 43:10, 55:8–9)

Truthful - All that God says is reality. Whether believed by man or not, whether seen as reality or not; if it is spoken by God, it is reality. Whatever He speaks becomes truth as we know it. (1 Samuel 15:29; Psalm 31:5; Titus 1:2; 1 John 5:20)

Wise - God's actions are based on His character which allows Him to choose righteous ends and to make fitting plans to achieve those ends. (Job 12:13; Isaiah 40:28; Daniel 2:20; James 3:17)

Wrathful - There is within God a hatred for all that is unrighteous and an unquenchable desire to punish all unrighteousness. Whatever is inconsistent with Him must ultimately be consumed. (Exodus 34:6–7; 2 Chronicles 19:2; Romans 1:18; Hebrews 10:30–31)

(Adapted from *Lord, I Want to Know You* by Kay Arthur.)

Appendix 2

Who I Am in Jesus Christ

I am the salt of the earth. (Matthew 5:13)

I am the light of the world. (Matthew 5:14)

I am a child of God, part of His family. (John 1:12; Romans 8:16)

I am part of the true vine, a channel of Christ's life. (John 15:1, 5)

I am Christ's friend. (John 15:15)

I am chosen and appointed by Christ to bear His fruit. (John 15:16)

I am a son of God. God is spiritually my Father. (Romans 8:14–15; Galatians 3:26; 4:6)

I am no longer under condemnation because I am in Christ. (Romans 8:1)

I am a joint-heir with Christ, sharing His inheritance with Him. (Romans 8:17)

I am accepted by Christ and belong in His family. (Romans 15:7; Ephesians 1:6)

I am sanctified, set apart for His use. (1 Corinthians 1:2)

I am a temple (home) of God. His Spirit (His life) dwells in me. (1 Corinthians 3:16; 6:19)

I am a member (part) of Christ's body. (1 Corinthians 12:27; Ephesians 5:30)

I am a new creation in Christ. (2 Corinthians 5:17)

I am reconciled to God and am an ambassador for Christ. (2 Corinthians 5:18–20)

I am the righteousness of God because of Christ. (2 Corinthians 5:21)

I am a son of God and one with other believers in Christ. (Galatians 3:26, 28)

I am an heir of God since I am a son of God. (Galatians 4:6, 7)

I am a saint. (1 Corinthians 1:2; Ephesians 1:1; Philippians 1:1; Colossians 1:2)

I am blessed with every spiritual blessing. (Ephesians 1:3)

I am chosen, holy and blameless before God. (Ephesians 1:4)

I am secure and sealed by the power of the Holy Spirit. (Ephesians 2:10)

I am God's workmanship (handiwork) created (born anew) in Christ to do His work that He planned beforehand that I should do. (Ephesians 2:10)

I am a fellow citizen with the rest of God's people in His family. (Ephesians 2:19)

I am righteous and holy. (Ephesians 4:24)

I am a citizen of heaven and seated in heaven right now. (Ephesians 2:6; Philippians 3:20)

I am hidden with Christ in God. (Colossians 3:3)

I am an expression of the life of Christ because He is my life. (Colossians 3:4)

I am chosen of God, holy, and dearly loved. (Colossians 3:12)

I am a son of light and not of darkness. (1 Thessalonians 5:5)

I am a partaker of Christ, I share in His life. (Hebrews 3:14)

I am one of God's living stones being built up (in Christ) as a spiritual house. (1 Peter 2:5)

I am a chosen race, a royal priesthood, a holy nation, a people for God's own possession to proclaim the excellencies of Him. (1 Peter 2:9–10)

I am an alien and stranger to this world I temporarily live in. (1 Peter 2:11)

I am an enemy of the devil. (1 Peter 5:8)

I am now a child of God. I will resemble Christ when He returns. (1 John 3:1–2)

I am born of God and the evil one (the devil) cannot touch me. (1 John 5:18)

(Adapted from *Living Free in Christ* by Neil Anderson.)

Appendix 3

Application and Discussion

These Vitamin A & D (application and discussion) exercises are designed to promote your ongoing interaction with Scripture in connection to the topics of the book. Use these for personal Bible study or group discussion.

Question 1: "Who is God?"

Vitamin A & D (Application and Discussion)
1. Read Exodus 3:1–14:9. In this encounter between God and Moses, what did God reveal about Himself? How did this revelation change the way Moses was going to live his life? How did God keep coming back to the issue of His own identity and power to give perspective to Moses? Similarly, how has God revealed Himself to you in your life? How has this changed the course of your existence here on earth?

2. Review Isaiah's encounter with God (Isaiah 6:1–8). Even though the passage is familiar, what do you observe about how Isaiah's view of God affected his sense of mission and direction in life? What did he understand about God and what specific difference did it seem to make in what he would do after this encounter?

3. Read Jeremiah chapter one. Again, here we see a man encountering the living God. Make a list of what God revealed to Jeremiah about His nature and character. What difference would that make for Jeremiah? What difference might these divine characteristics make in the way you serve God, work on the job, relate to others, etc.?

4. Read Daniel 4:28–37. Here is a powerful, self-directed man whose encounter with God jolted his perspective of himself and his life. Make a "before" and "after" column and write down the words or ideas that contrast Nebuchadnezzar's "before" and "after" understanding of the true God? Looking around society, how do you see people living in the "before" column or the "after" column, based on their theology?

5. Read Acts 8:1–3 along with Acts 9:1–19 and Acts 26:1–23. What did Paul come to understand about God? Make a list of the ways in which his life and direction changed as a result. Do you have a similar grasp of purpose and mission? If not, is there some sense in which you need a more real and life-changing view of God? How can you achieve this?

Question 2: "Who am I?"

Vitamin A & D (Application and Discussion)

1. Read 2 Corinthians 4:16–5:10. Here Paul is reflecting on the difference between our "external" identity and our "essential" identity. What differences does he note? Speaking from the perspective of his "essential" identity, what purposes and perspectives does he embrace? How about you? How much of your life is lived focusing on the external you and those purposes versus the essential you and the goals of that dimension? Does anything need to change?

2. Continue with Paul as he describes how his new life in Christ affects his motives and objectives. Based upon 2 Corinthians 5:11–15, what seems to now matter to this man of clear identity? What now motivates him? How does this compare to the average person in society today in terms of how one's sense of identity motivates and guides his or her life?

3. Going on to 5:16–21, how does Paul's new life affect the way he sees other people? With this new perspective, what does he feel compelled to do about it and why? What words does Paul use in this passage to describe himself? How might you correlate this self-view with the perspectives and objectives noted here?

4. In 6:1–2, Paul urges the Corinthians to receive God's fullest grace for their lives, even as Paul had. Review his commentary in the previous two chapters (four and five) and make a list of the ways in which God's grace was active in his life—clarifying identity, sustaining clear purpose, motivating and enabling Paul. In comparison to this, are you receiving God's grace in vain? If so, pray for a fuller understanding and experience in light of the following verses (1 Corinthians 15:10; 2 Corinthians 1:12; Titus 2:10–11; 1 Peter 4:10).

5. Psychologists and sociologists note the tremendous need for people to be loved, accepted, understood and valued. Yet, read Paul's account of his own experiences in 6:3–10. Are these experiences of being loved, understood, accepted, and valued? How did he respond? Did he feel rejected or compelled to retaliate? What was the source of his response to these things based upon what has been seen in previous verses? Are there any truths here that need to be applied on a daily basis to your way of thinking? What are they? How can you renew your mind daily to change your thinking?

Question 3: "Why am I here?"

Vitamin A & D (Application and Discussion)
1. Read the following verses that describe Christ's mission here on earth: Matthew 5:17–18, 20:28; Mark 10:45; Luke 4:43,

12:49–51, 19:10; John 6:38, 9:39, 10:10, 12:27, 12:46–47, 18:37; and 1 Timothy 1:15. With these thoughts in mind, what do you think might be applicable to the one who claims to be a follower of Christ in this life? What elements of this mission do you feel you should more fully embrace and follow?

2. Your purpose and mission should be based upon the Scriptures. Here are a few verses to consider. Proverbs 30:7–9; Ecclesiastes 12:13; Micah 6:8; Matthew 6:33, 22:37–40, 28:19–20; John 4:34, 15:1–27, 17:4; Acts 1:8, 20:24; 1 Corinthians 10:31; Ephesians 2:10; Philippians 3:10. Create a one- or two-sentence "rough draft" of a mission statement that might flow from the ideas of these verses.

3. Read Proverbs 16:4. Why do you feel Christians sometimes want to fulfill someone else's purpose? What problems does that create? How may it affect our attitude? How does it affect the "body" as a whole?

4. Read Ephesians 2:10 and Philippians 2:13. Make a list of those works that you feel God would want you to do based on your gifts, interests, abilities, personality, and experiences. What does this do to your motivation, knowing that all these

areas can be used for God's purpose? What thoughts do you have concerning the passage in Philippians, relative to your works?

5. Read Romans 14:12 and 1 Corinthians 3:10–15. If you were to suddenly stand before the Lord, what are the things that you would be able to put on your account that would be a fulfillment of God's purpose for your life? What changes would you want to make in your present activities?

Question 4: "What really matters?"

Vitamin A & D (Application and Discussion)
1. Review Exodus 20:1–17. Here we see the Lord giving to Israel (and to all who would know and follow Him) a set of principles by which to live. Review these and take a few moments to write, in your own words, a philosophy statement based upon these fundamental precepts. It doesn't have to be a perfect rendition. Just write out a summary statement that makes sense to you. How do you actually embrace this statement in your lifestyle? Would you say this is part of your personal philosophy of life?

2. Review the Sermon on the Mount found in Matthew, chapters five through seven. Make a note of the core principles Jesus is espousing here. Then, put those core thoughts together in a summary statement. Would you say that this statement is a valid philosophy for your life? Which elements of it are you actually practicing? Which do you need to embrace more fully?

3. Read the story in Luke 10:25–37. On a piece of paper (or on a white board if you are in a group) make a list of the key players in this story. Now, based upon their described actions, what do you think are some of the main elements of each person's philosophy of life? How does their apparent philosophy differ from first impressions based on appearance or title? Can you think of times when your actual philosophy showed in your actions, even though you may have created a different impression toward others by external means?

4. Read Matthew 19:16–24. What was this man's stated philosophy? What was his actual philosophy? Was there any apparent disparity? How do you see this same problem in people's lives today? How about your own life?

5. Review Paul's message to the Ephesian elders in Acts 20:17–35. This is one of his most potent statements about ministry. As you have done on previous questions, isolate the core principles he gives here and then put them together in a "philosophy of ministry" statement. How can you minister to others in a more effective way by embracing this philosophy?

Question 5: "What shall I do?"

Vitamin A & D (Application and Discussion)
1. Read Mark 8:34–38. According to this passage, how might potential followers of Christ misplace their own priorities? What result did Jesus predict? How do you see people today falling into the trap of misplaced priorities as Jesus describes it here? Do you ever see "Christians" doing this? How can they avoid this pitfall?

2. Read Matthew 6:19–24. What warning did Jesus give here about wrong priorities? What dilemma would people face that chose this pathway of wrong priorities? What did He suggest they do to deal with the problem? Do you think the average Christian today is really committed to this kind of obedient living? Why or why not?

3. Continue reading this section by noting Matthew 6:25–34. What did our Lord challenge us to NOT focus on? Why did He say this? Do you order your priorities in this way? How might your lifestyle and priorities change today in order to reflect a strong adherence to Matthew 6:33?

4. Read the account of the Prodigal Son in Luke 15:8–22. How did the priorities of this young man become confused? What result did his decisions create? What did it take for him to reassess? In what way do you find people today playing the role of the Prodigal in their own decision-making processes, and what does it usually take to get them to reassess? What warning and reassurance does Psalm 32:2–10 give on this issue?

5. Read Luke 12:13–21. Here is a man who asked himself the question, "What shall I do . . .?" Did he select the right priority? Why or why not? In what way do his choices reflect the thinking of our own society? What kind of warning might this passage give to today's Christian?

Question 6: "How shall I do it?"

Vitamin A & D (Application and Discussion)

1. Read Nehemiah chapters 1 and 2. What specific goal had God established in Nehemiah's heart? Now, review the passage to see what kind of theology Nehemiah embraced (note 1:4–11). How did he view himself? What words does Nehemiah use? How did his theology and identity affect his goal? How does your theology and identity affect your goals?

2. Continuing in these first two chapters of Nehemiah, why do you suppose Nehemiah was not content just to remain in Persia with King Artaxerxes? Based on the account, what kind of purpose statement might fit Nehemiah's life as his overarching objective for living? What pursuits did he reject in order to accomplish this mission? In what way have you exemplified this same kind of focus?

3. Again, from the same account, can you find any guiding principles or convictions, which Nehemiah held? What beliefs did he seem to have about how he should implement his vision? Try to make a list of the ones that are most apparent? Can you find other Scripture verses that would confirm the validity of these beliefs?

4. Finally, from Nehemiah, note again the major goal Nehemiah embraced. What minor goals did he seem to identify that would help accomplish the main task? What other feature of his goal do you note from 2:6b? What was the outcome (note 6:15–16)? What goals do you have that could have a similar impact?

5. Read John 17:1–18. Here, Christ reflects on the objective and accomplishments of His ministry. Note how verses 1–5 speak of His purpose of glorifying the Father and the mission of bringing eternal life. He felt he had completed this mission. From the following verses (6–18) what goals had been accomplished to achieve this sense of completion? What can you learn from the deliberate nature of his life as you clarify His goals for your life?

Question 7: "When shall I do it?"

Vitamin A & D (Application and Discussion)
1. Read Mark 1:21–35. List the various activities that Jesus was involved in on this particular Sabbath day in Capernaum. How did Jesus maintain a right attitude in the midst of such a high priority on spending time with His Father? Are you taking sufficient time to meet with God, and to get His direction and power for your life and ministry?

Appendix 3 243

2. Read John 4:8, 30–36. What does this account reveal about Jesus' priorities? What do Jesus' words (verses 34–36) teach us about our priorities? How well do your plans for today reflect the priorities of Jesus? What specific changes do you need to make in today's schedule to order your life around eternal priorities?

3. Read John 9:4–5. How did the realization of the shortness of His time on earth affect Jesus? What are "the works of God" that Jesus fulfilled while He was here on earth? What are some of the works God wants to accomplish through you during your time here on earth? How can you use your time today to do "the works of Him who has sent Me"?

4. Read Matthew 14:1–23. What was the occasion for Jesus' going away to the desert (Matthew 14:10–13; Mark 6:30–31)? As a man, describe what may have been Jesus' emotional and physical condition at the time. How did Jesus respond when the multitudes interrupted His "private retreat" (Matthew 14:14; Mark 6:33–34)? How did Jesus use the lateness of the hour (Matthew 14:15) to manifest the glory of God? How did Jesus compensate for the time alone that had been interrupted (Matthew 14:23)? How did you respond the last time someone infringed on time that you had set aside as personal time? What pressure on your time are you currently facing that could be transformed into an opportunity to glorify God?

5. Read John 11:1–10, 18–26, 38–45. Humanly speaking, what were some of the disadvantages of Jesus' waiting two days to go to Lazarus' home? What blessings and benefits occurred because Jesus was sensitive to God's perfect timing? What activities are on your "urgent" list that God may want you to wait to accomplish so He can receive greater glory? What activities are you delaying that God may want you to do immediately?

Notes

Introduction: Choosing the Right Approach

1. Quoted by Gloria Naylor in *More Reflections on the Meaning of Life* (Boston: Little, Brown and Company, 1992), 10.

2. Quoted by Stephen Covey in *The Seven Habits of Highly Effective People* (New York: Simon & Schuster, 1989), 294.

3. *Reader's Digest* (January, 1995), 68.

4. Quoted by Stephen Covey in *The Seven Habits of Highly Effective People*, 294.

5. Morris, Tom, *True Success* (New York: Grosset/Putnam, 1994), 35.

6. Quoted by John Roger and Peter McWilliams in *Do It! Let's Get off Our Buts* (Los Angeles: Prelude Press, 1991), 240.

7. Grizzard, Lewis, Ibid., 51.

8. Wilmington, Harold, *Wilmington's Guide to the Bible* (Wheaton: Tyndale, 1985), 136.

9. Quoted by John Maxwell in *Be All You Can Be* (Wheaton, Ill.: Victor Books, 1987), 166.

10. Carter, Stephen, *Integrity* (New York: Basic Books, 1996), 7.

11. Morris, *True Success*, 37.

12. Quoted by John Maxwell in *Developing the Leader Within You* (Nashville: Thomas Nelson, 1993), 130.

13. Covey, Stephen, *The Seven Habits of Highly Effective People*, 95.

Question 1: "Who is God?"

1. Tozer, A. W., *The Knowledge of the Holy* (New York: Harper & Row, 1961), 12.

2. Guinness, Os, *God in the Dark* (Wheaton: Crossway, 1996), 61.

3. Connolly, Cyril, as quoted in *Do It! Let's Get Off Our Buts*, 248.

4. Quoted by Tom Peters in *True Success*, 38.

5. Chopra, Deepak, *The Seven Spiritual Laws of Success*—audio version (Amber-Allen/New World Library, 1997).

6. As cited by Marcus J. Borg in *The God We Never Knew* (San Francisco: HarperCollins, 1997), 24.

7. Quoted by Tom Morris in *True Success*, 41.

8. Stafford, Tim, *Knowing the Face of God* (Grand Rapids: Zondervan Publishing House, 1986), 25.

Question 2: "Who am I?"

1. Quoted by John Roger and Peter Mc Williams in *Do It! Let's Get off Our Buts*, 62.

2. As cited by Robert S. McGee in *The Search for Significance* (Houston: Rapha, 1990), 14.

3. Ibid., 14.

4. Needham, David, *Birthright: Christian, Do You Know Who You Are?* (Portland: Multnomah Press, 1979), 25.

5. Gillham, Bill, *Lifetime Guarantee* (Eugene, Ore.: Harvest House Publishers, 1993), 72.

6. Needham, David, 47.

7. I am indebted to Pastor Rick Warren, Saddleback Church, Mission Viejo, Calif., for clarifying many of these concepts through his "S.H.A.P.E." acrostic.

Question 3: "Why am I here?"

1. Munroe, Myles, *In Pursuit of Purpose* (Shippensburg, Penn.: Destiny Image Publishers, 1992), i.

2. Quoted by Oswald Sanders in *Spiritual Leadership* (Chicago: Moody Press, 1980), 135.

3. Munroe, Myles, 1.

4. Ibid., vii.

5. Ibid., vii.

6. Morley, Patrick, *Man in the Mirror*, 60.

7. Bach, Richard, as quoted in *Do It! Let's Get Off Our Buts*, 144.

8. Munroe, Myles, *In Pursuit of Purpose*, 7.

9. Covey, Stephen, *The Seven Habits of Highly Effective People*, 107–108.

10. Shelley, Mary Wollstonecraft, as quoted in *Do It! Let's Get Off Our Buts*, 140.

11. Quoted by Tom Morris in *True Success*, 278.

Question 4: "What really matters?"

1. Harrison, F. C., *Spirit of Leadership: Inspiring Quotations for Leaders* (Germantown, Tenn.: Leadership, Education, and Development, 1989), 3.

2. Harrison, F. C., *Spirit of Leadership*, 3.

3. As cited by Linda and Richard Byre in *Teaching Your Children Values* (New York: Simon and Schuster, 1993), 12.

4. Gallup News Organization, NBC News Poll, January 31, 1998.

5. Lewis, Hunter, *A Question of Values* (San Francisco: Harper SF, 1991), 12.

6. Quoted by John Maxwell in *Developing the Leader Within You*, 32.

7. Ibid., 29.

8. Nee, Watchman, *Not I, but Christ* (New York: Christian Fellowship, 1974), 64.

9. MacDonald, Gordon, at a "Mastering Ministry" conference; January, 1993.

10. Maxwell, John, *Developing the Leader Within You*, 24–25.

11. Forbes, Malcolm, with Jeff Bloch, *What Happened to Their Kids?* (New York: Simon & Schuster, 1990), 237–239.

Question 5: "What should I do?"

1. Baruch, Bernard, as quoted by Charles Swindoll in *Come Before Winter* (Portland: Multnomah Press, 1985), 23.

2. Maxwell, John, *Developing the Leader Within You*, 20.

3. Covey, Stephen, *First Things First* (New York: Simon & Schuster, 1994), 39.

4. Cook, William H., *Success, Motivation, and the Scriptures* (Nashville: Broadman, 1974), 127.

5. McKenzie, E. C., *Mac's Giant Book of Quips and Quotes* (Eugene, Ore.: Harvest House, 1980), 76.

6. Ibid., 76.

7. Cited by John Maxwell in *Developing the Leader Within You*, 28.

8. Ibid., 25–26.

9. As cited by Ann Landers in *The Mercury News*, May 10, 1984.

10. Swindoll, Charles, *Come Before Winter* (Portland: Multnomah Press, 1985), 24.

11. Morley, Patrick, 164.

12. John Maxwell, *Developing the Leader Within You*, 27.

13. Wayne Martindale and Jerry Root, ed., *The Quotable Lewis* (Wheaton: Tyndale House, 1989), 496.

14. Frost, Robert, *Structure, Sound, and Sense* (New York: Harcourt, Brace, Jovanovich, 1974), 629.

Question 6: "How should I do it"?

1. Gordon, David, *Spirit of Leadership*, 260.

2. Quoted by John Maxwell in *The Success Journey* (Nashville: Thomas Nelson, 1997), 87.

3. Proverbs 16:4.

4. Maxwell, John, *Be All You Can Be* (Wheaton: Victor Books, 1987), 68.

5. Morris, Tom, *True Success*, 217.

6. Ibid., 217–218.

7. Maxwell, John, *Be All You Can Be* (Wheaton: Victor Books, 1987), 61.

8. Ibid., 62.

Question 7: "When should I do it?"

1. Martindale, Wayne and Jerry Root, *The Quotable Lewis* (Wheaton: Tyndale, 1989), 580.

2. Knight, Walter B., *Knight's Treasury of 2,000 Illustrations* (Grand Rapids: Eerdmans, 1963), 407.

3. Swenson, Richard, *Margin* (Colorado Springs, Colo.: NavPress, 1992), 145.

4. Bill Mills, speaking at the CBA of Northern California/ Nevada Annual meetings, Asilomar, Calif., February 1998.

5. Habit, need more information here.

6. Quoted by Daniel J. Boorstein in *The Discoverers* (New York: Random House, 1983), 25.

7. Gibbs, Nancy, "How America Has Run Out of Time," *Time*, April 24, 1989, 59.

8. Shumacher, E.F., *Good Work* (New York: Harper & Row, 1979), 25.

9. Swenson, 153.

10. Meade, Frank S., *12,000 Religious Quotations* (Grand Rapids: Baker, 1989), 442.

11. Sanders, J. Oswald, *Spiritual Leadership* (Chicago: Moody Press, 1970), 90.

12. Meade, Frank S., *12,000 Religious Quotations*, 443.

13. MacArthur, John, *New Testament Commentary on Ephesians* (Chicago: Moody, 1986), 222.

14. Martindale, Wayne and Jerry Root, *The Quotable Lewis*, 580.

15. Edwards, Jonathan, *The Works of Jonathan Edwards*, rev. Edward Hickman (1834 reprint, Edinburgh, Scotland: The Banner of Truth Trust, 1974), xxi.

16. Swindoll, Charles, *The Quest for Character* (Portland: Multnomah Press, 1987), 119–124.

17. MacArthur, *New Testament Commentary on Ephesians* (Chicago: Moody, 1986), 222.

18. Swenson, 149.

19. Fehsenfeld, Del, *Spirit of Revival Buchanan Michigan* (Life Action Ministries, November 1986), 2.

Epilogue

1. Martindale, Wayne and Jerry Root, *The Quotable Lewis*, 241.

2. Author unknown.

Correspondence

Tapes and study guides for "The Seven Most Important Questions You'll Ever Answer" are available at the address below. Please write to

Daniel Henderson
Arcade Baptist Church
3927 Marconi Avenue
Sacremento, CA 95821

or visit the website at
http://www.strategicrenewal.com

Note to the Reader